T0360772

Strategy Beyond Markets

All businesses operate under a set of rules – laws and regulations – that occasionally require updating. Improving these "rules of the competitive game" can, sometimes, be vital for a business or industry to survive. *Strategy Beyond Markets* explains how the rules of the competitive game are changed, and what role the business sector can play in this change. Through the analysis of case studies, a new discipline called Strategy Beyond Markets is presented. It studies how business regulations – taxes, subsidies, compliance rules, production and marketability standards, and licensing requirements – come about, and why they take certain forms. This discipline helps businesses operate effectively in the politico-regulatory arenas where the rules of the competitive game are made. Strategy Beyond Markets complements, but is fundamentally different from, the traditional discipline of Competitive Strategy.

Nicola Persico is a professor at Northwestern University. Previously, he has been a professor at UCLA, the University of Pennsylvania, and NYU. He was awarded the inaugural Carlo Alberto Medal for the best Italian economist under the age of forty, and he is a fellow of the Econometric Society.

Strategy Beyond Markets

Political Economy from the Firm's Perspective

NICOLA PERSICO
Northwestern University

CAMBRIDGE
UNIVERSITY PRESS

CAMBRIDGE
UNIVERSITY PRESS

Shaftesbury Road, Cambridge CB2 8EA, United Kingdom

One Liberty Plaza, 20th Floor, New York, NY 10006, USA

477 Williamstown Road, Port Melbourne, VIC 3207, Australia

314–321, 3rd Floor, Plot 3, Splendor Forum, Jasola District Centre, New Delhi – 110025, India

103 Penang Road, #05–06/07, Visioncrest Commercial, Singapore 238467

Cambridge University Press is part of Cambridge University Press & Assessment, a department of the University of Cambridge.

We share the University's mission to contribute to society through the pursuit of education, learning and research at the highest international levels of excellence.

www.cambridge.org

Information on this title: www.cambridge.org/9781009393713

DOI: 10.1017/9781009393744

First published 2024

A catalogue record for this publication is available from the British Library

Library of Congress Cataloging-in-Publication Data
NAMES: Persico, Nicola Giuseppe, 1967– author.
TITLE: Strategy beyond markets : political economy from the firm's perspective / Nicola Giuseppe Persico, Northwestern University, Illinois.
DESCRIPTION: 1 Edition. | New York : Cambridge University Press, 2024. | Includes bibliographical references and index.
IDENTIFIERS: LCCN 2023005188 (print) | LCCN 2023005189 (ebook) | ISBN 9781009393713 (hardback) | ISBN 9781009393744 (ebook)
SUBJECTS: LCSH: Entrepreneurship – Government policy. | Business enterprises – Law and legislation. | Strategic planning.
CLASSIFICATION: LCC HB615 .P3934 2024 (print) | LCC HB615 (ebook) | DDC 338/.04–dc23/eng/20230428
LC record available at https://lccn.loc.gov/2023005188
LC ebook record available at https://lccn.loc.gov/2023005189

ISBN 978-1-009-39371-3 Hardback
ISBN 978-1-009-39373-7 Paperback

Contents

Figures

Tables

Preface

Strategy Beyond Markets (SBM) is the discipline that studies how business regulations come about and why they take certain forms and not others. Business regulations include: taxes, subsidies, compliance rules, production and marketability standards, licensing requirements, and many others.

Business practitioners have at least two concerns regarding business regulations. First, is a change in regulation likely and, if so, in what direction? Second, can my company or industry have input into the change? Chapters 3–10 provide insights into these two questions.

This book will mostly focus on SBM as a tool for creating and capturing value. The issue of whether SBM is a good way for business to operate in society is not the focus of this book: It is addressed only in Chapter 11.

Chapter 12 compares and contrasts the principles of SBM with those of Competitive Strategy. The disciplines of SBM and Competitive Strategy share the same goals: value maximization and value capture. But the locus of analysis is different: the legislative and regulatory arena in the former case and the market in the latter case.

As an academic field, SBM draws from a number of other fields that study how resource allocation is affected by political and business actors. In addition to Competitive Strategy, these fields include: political economy, political science, and industrial organization. This book borrows from these academic fields, but it aspires to be more practical. It takes the perspective of the business practitioner – the owner or the CEO – and translates academic knowledge into business-relevant prescriptions.

Finally, this book is almost exclusively focused on the US. Other political systems are treated only briefly and for the sake of comparison.

Acknowledgments

This textbook is written for the students in the Strategy Beyond Markets class at the Kellogg School of Management, which I teach. The class, and this textbook, contribute to bringing the study of regulation into business education. This program was pioneered by David Baron of Stanford University whose textbook, *Business and Its Environment*, remains a classic. I owe Baron a large, albeit indirect, intellectual debt. I owe, also, a big debt of gratitude to Daniel Diermeier, who trained me in the subject, and to Tim Feddersen.

This textbook is largely focused on the United States. Although I discuss other political systems, including nondemocracies, I do so only briefly and for the sake of comparison.

Additional thanks to Herschel Cutler, Paul Doucette, Georgy Egorov, Ivana Jemelkova, Charlene MacDonald, and Nicola Scocchi. I am grateful to the students who spotted some typos in the manuscript's early drafts, including Pushkaran Palani and Hannah Weingold.

A disclaimer: Occasionally, the nature of the subject matter causes me to portray individuals, companies, and even governments, in a light that may be perceived as unflattering. This comes with the territory. There is never any value judgment implied on classes of people, industries, countries, or nationalities.

I

Introduction

In the early days of Microsoft, I prided myself on how little time we spent talking to people in the federal government. I would tell people: isn't it great that we can be successful and not even have an office in DC? As I learned the hard way ... this was not a wise position to take. Staying on the sidelines wasn't just a mistake for our company – it was a mistake for the industry.... Microsoft and other tech companies needed to engage more with leaders in the United States, Europe, and elsewhere. My days of bragging about not having an office in DC were over.

Bill Gates.[1]

This chapter explains what Strategy beyond Markets is, and why it is important to business practitioners.

1.1 WHAT IS STRATEGY BEYOND MARKETS?

Because Strategy beyond Markets is not a standard part of business education, it is helpful to provide a definition. Here is mine.

Definition 1 (Strategy beyond Markets, or SBM) *Strategy beyond Markets (SBM) is the discipline that studies how a business pursues long-term value creation and capture by advocating for business-related policy agendas.*

This book seeks to guide business leaders as they engage in the practices covered by Definition 1. Next, I comment on the definition. A *policy* is a set of rules under which society, including particularly the business

---

[1] Foreword to Smith and Browne (2021).

sector, operates. SBM focuses on those rules that are set by legislatures and by regulatory bodies such as government agencies or ministries. The *agenda* is the specific set of rules that a business or industry would like to be enacted at a given moment.

The *advocacy* mentioned in Definition 1 is the interaction between a business or industry and the institutions that make policy, that is, with legislatures and regulatory bodies. A formal definition follows.

Definition 2 (Business Advocacy)   *Business advocacy is the creation of coalitions of interests as described in Chapters 4 and 5, and the communication of persuasive information as described in Chapters 6 and 7, in the pursuit of business-related policy agendas.*

Business advocacy is the way that business interests operate in the political arena, and is described in detail in Chapters 4 and 7. Business advocacy is *strategic* because its consequences are difficult to undo: Once the rules of the game are set by elected officials or regulators, they tend to stay in place for a long time. This is why the word "strategy" appears in this book's title.

Definitions 1 and 2 restrict attention to *business-related* policy agendas. By this I mean a desired change (or lack thereof) in the laws and regulations that control value creation and capture, that is, in the taxes, subsidies, compliance rules, production and marketability standards, licensing requirements, and many others besides, that are *closely related to the firm's own business goals*. This is in contrast with the notion of corporate activism proposed in Section 11.3, which has broader social goals beyond the firm's own business goals. This book will not focus on the pursuit of broader social goals. Nevertheless, some of the prescriptions in this book can also be applied in the pursuit of these goals.

This book takes a positive perspective, not a normative one. Primarily, this is not a book about what firms *should* do vis-à-vis society: It is a book about how the firm can interact effectively with legislators and regulators in order to *maximize long-term value*. The only partial exception is Chapter 11, where I discuss the role of SBM in society.

I will use the term "policy entrepreneur" to indicate a person, or organization, that advocates for a policy agenda.

Definition 3 (Policy Entrepreneur)   *A policy entrepreneur is a person or organization that advocates for a policy agenda.*

Policy entrepreneurs are agents who are "willing to invest their resources in return for future policies they favor."[2] These agents can be businesses, lobbyists, trade associations, NGOs, and so on. Agents who engage in business advocacy are, by definition, policy entrepreneurs.

Besides Definition 1, another way of defining SBM is by contrast with Competitive Strategy. The two disciplines share the same goal: to maximize value creation and value capture. But whereas Competitive Strategy takes market and competitive structures as exogenous, SBM views these structures as endogenous, that is, as the result of intentional actions taken beyond the market. SBM recognizes that laws and regulations are the "deep fundamentals" that give rise to a given market and competitive structure and, at the same time, views these deep fundamentals as objects of strategic management. I will return to this point in Chapter 12.

1.2 WHY SBM IS IMPORTANT TO CEOS – AND WHY YOU SHOULD READ THIS BOOK

This book's content is important to managers, investors, and startup owners.

Useful for CEOs and General Managers   Every year, the consulting company PricewaterhouseCoopers surveys the CEOs of large companies and ask about "potential economic, policy, social, environmental and business threats to your organisation's growth prospects." Table 1.1 reports the top-most threat in the years since 2015. In most years, the top-most concern has been overregulation. Table 1.1 indicates that SBM is a top priority for many CEOs.

Furthermore, SBM can be a useful tool for managers who head up a product or business line, even if they are not (yet) CEOs, if the product or business line they are responsible for has regulatory implications (see, e.g., the cryptocurrency minicase at page 33) or is threatened with disruptive regulation (see, e.g., the e-cigarette case in Section 2.5).

Useful for Investors   Investors can benefit from predicting whether market actors will be able to successfully operate in the beyond-market arena. For example, the entire recycling industry was exposed to prolonged existential risk in the Recyclers case presented in Section 2.2. At the time of

---

[2] Kingdon (1984), p. 214.

TABLE 1.1 *Top threat to "your organization's growth prospects," by year.*

Year	Top threat to growth
2015	Overregulation
2016	Overregulation
2017	Uncertain economic growth
2018	Overregulation
2019	Overregulation
2020	Overregulation
2021	Pandemic

Source: 2015–21 PwC's Annual Global CEO Surveys.

this case, an investor might have been interested in forecasting whether the recycling industry would survive the crisis. In the end, the industry's SBM succeeded and the recycling industry survived. In contrast, the outgoing-telemarketing industry fell victim to a regulatory crisis and did not recover, as discussed at page 118. Investors should use SBM to forecast whether an industry will be able to pull through a legislative or regulatory crisis.

Useful for Startup Owners/Founders Many startups operate in a regulatory gray area because their products and services are new and, therefore, unregulated. This ambiguity creates risk and opportunities. In Section 2.5, JUUL, an innovative startup, failed to recognize that its SBM should focus on industry-level self-regulation and, as a result, was punishingly regulated by the government. By contrast, the pharmaceutical startup Sprout executed an SBM that, although Machiavellian, made the owners very rich: See Section 2.7.

1.3 SBM: THE MOST IMPORTANT SUBJECT YOU'VE NEVER HEARD OF

Given its practical importance, it is perhaps surprising that SBM is not more central to business education and, more generally, to business discourse. I believe this is partly because business executives, and even professional lobbyists, are reluctant to publicly discuss their advocacy efforts and even their major SBM achievements. I attribute this reluctance to the fear of being perceived as Machiavellian by the general public. As a result, SBM often seems to take place behind a veil of secrecy.

As a political economist, my view of business advocacy is more positive than most people's. I see some societal benefits in business advocacy, as well as some drawbacks. In the United States, on the whole, the societal benefits seem to me to exceed the drawbacks: I will make this case in Chapter 11. From my perspective, then, business advocacy is a social net-positive.

In any case, regardless of whether SBM is viewed as a net-positive or a net-negative, it is a lawful practice and it cannot be stopped. Therefore, it is better that SBM be discussed openly than that it be practiced in the proverbial smoke-filled rooms. Else, how can best practices in business advocacy ever be established? Besides, smoke-filled rooms are increasingly rare nowadays, so businesses must be prepared to publicly defend their SBM in a way that withstands scrutiny. By providing a conceptual framework for SBM, a technical language, and case studies, this book seeks to lift the veil of secrecy that shrouds SBM.

2

Illustrative Examples

Just because you do not take an interest in politics doesn't mean politics
won't take an interest in you.
Pericles (attributed)

In each of the following sections a business, or an industry, was forced
to use SBM to deal with a risk or seize an opportunity. Some succeeded;
some failed. Each section illustrates one or more specific learning points:
The learning points are mentioned at the end of each section. The chapter's overall message is that SBM can be crucial to value creation or
destruction.

2.1 VOLCKER RULE

The 2008 financial crisis was perceived, at the time, as the most severe
downturn in the United States since the Great Depression. US GDP failed
to grow in 2008, and it shrank by more than 2 percent in the following
year. Unemployment shot up from 5 to 10 percent.

The causes of the crisis were complex and, to this day, are somewhat
controversial. The crisis started in the mortgage market, where many
mortgages had been taken out by low-income borrowers. These mortgage
contracts had been packaged into complex financial securities that were
widely held and considered relatively safe, despite the risk of default on
the underlying mortgages. As low-income borrowers started to default
more often, the financial system collectively took stock of the amount
of risk contained in these securities, and was seized by fear. This fear
led to the bankruptcy of the storied trading house Lehman Brothers in
September 2008.

The US government intentionally let Lehman fail. However, the government's inaction triggered a market panic that, eventually, forced the government to bail out other larger financial institutions to the tune of tens of billions of dollars. The insurance company AIG received $67 billion, Bank of America and Citigroup received $45 billion each, and so on.[1]

Ordinary citizens were outraged at the use of hard-earned taxpayers' dollars to bail out the very institutions that had created the crisis. Grassroots political movements that objected to the bailouts, such as *Occupy Wall Street* on the left and the *Tea Party* on the right, grew rapidly. They sponsored candidates for elected office who, if elected, would oppose bailing out the financial industry.

A narrative emerged: Large financial firms had taken on excessive risks based on the expectation that the government would bail them out if they got into trouble. According to this narrative, large financial firms knew they were "too big to fail" and took advantage. This narrative resulted in proposed regulation, called the Volcker Rule, that threatened to forbid large financial firms from investing their own capital in financial markets – the so-called "proprietary trading." This rule would reduce the financial firms' incentives to take on financial risk. The rule was named after Paul Volcker, the legendary central banker who had first proposed it. It seemed especially important to apply this rule to banks, because banks were *explicitly* insured against bankruptcy by the government through the FDIC.[2] This protection from bankruptcy arguably made banks excessively willing to take risks.

Some respected economists in the Obama administration doubted that the Volcker Rule would do much good, and they thought that it would be difficult to administer.[3] However, the proposal was publicly supported by financial regulators, including five former Secretaries of the Treasury in a letter to the *Wall Street Journal*. Thus, the Volcker Rule was added to a larger bill named the Dodd–Frank Act that was making its way through Congress.

---

[1] See Kiel and Nguyen (2021).
[2] FDIC stands for Federal Deposit Insurance Corporation. Banks are required to contribute to the FDIC against the risk of a run on deposits. The very existence of the FDIC had made bank runs rare, which was the desired effect. However, it had the unintended consequence of making banks immune to bankruptcy.
[3] Cassidy (2010).

Banks, large and small, opposed the Volcker Rule. It was estimated that, by banning proprietary trading, the Volcker Rule would cost large banks about 10 percent of total trading revenues.[4] Small banks opposed the Volcker Rule, and the Dodd–Frank Act generally, because it increased the regulatory burden. However, given the political climate at the time, opposing the Volcker Rule would be an uphill battle for the financial industry.

Lobbying legislators to withdraw the Volcker Rule was a long shot. The public mood across the country was ominous, and President Obama had put the financial industry on notice: "[W]hat we've seen so far, in recent weeks, is an army of industry lobbyists from Wall Street descending on Capitol Hill to try and block basic and common-sense rules of the road that would protect our economy and the American people. So if these folks want a fight, it's a fight I'm ready to have."[5]

Still, lacking a better option, the financial industry did attempt to lobby legislators. The effort, however, was ultimately unsuccessful. The Dodd–Frank Act, including the Volcker Rule, was eventually enacted in 2010.[6] Its subsequent implementation, however, was majorly delayed: Government regulators faced a complex set of choices, and they were lobbied by industry representatives in more than 1,400 separate meetings on the Volcker Rule.[7] The notice of proposed rulemaking ended up running to an amazing 530 pages. In the final version, regulators allowed a series of exceptions. Finally, the Volcker Rule went into effect in 2015, but with some compliance deadlines extended up to 2017. In 2020, financial regulators revisited and further pared back the Volcker Rule.

Learning Points This case illustrates that an industry can have influence with regulators even if it is deeply unpopular with the public at large and, therefore, with politicians. This influence stems, in part, from the industry's superior knowledge of the unintended consequences of regulation. In the Volcker Rule's case, the unintended consequences were that banks would stop acting as market makers in certain securities, thus reducing the liquidity in these markets.[8] Chapter 7 discusses regulators.

---

[4] Minor and Persico (2012), p. 3.
[5] Obama (2010).
[6] The Volcker Rule is Section 619 of the Dodd–Frank Act.
[7] Krawiec and Liu (2015).
[8] At the time I am writing, it is controversial whether the Volcker Rule actually decreased liquidity: Allahrakha et al. (2019) find that it did, whereas Trebbi and Xiao (2019) reach a different conclusion.

2.2 RECYCLERS

The director of the trade association of US scrap recyclers (Institute of Scrap Recycling Industries, or ISRI) picked up the phone. At the other end of the line, a widow was sobbing and asking for his help. The small recycling business she had inherited from her husband had just been notified that it was responsible for millions of dollars in "Superfund" cleanup costs at a far-away industrial site. Superfund was the colloquial name for an environmental remediation program established by a relatively new law, the Comprehensive Environmental Response, Compensation, and Liability Act of 1980. She was flabbergasted: Many years before, her business had indeed supplied that industrial site with recycled iron but not with any hazardous waste. If required to pay, her business would go bankrupt.[9]

That week, several other ISRI members called in with the same problem: They had supplied recycled raw materials to some industrial sites in the past and now, out of nowhere, they were being hit with astronomical Superfund cleanup bills. ISRI's director was dumbfounded: The Superfund law was about ensuring that polluters pay the costs of cleaning up old industrial sites. But why would supplying recycled metal be equated with polluting an industrial site? The director scrambled to figure out what was going on.

After making inquiries, he learned that these problems originated from a Pennsylvania judge's interpretation of legislative language. According to the Superfund law, those who had "arranged for the disposal or treatment of hazardous waste" at Superfund sites were responsible for the cleanup costs, whether or not their waste had caused the pollution. This fateful reference to "waste" was actually a typographical error – a leftover from a previous draft that wasn't supposed to appear in the final version of the law. However, it did. This solitary mention of "waste" caused the recycling industry to be dragged into the orbit of Superfund because, based on other preexisting statutory language, the judge had deemed that recycled materials were classified as "waste," and so the recyclers had to be responsible for the cleanup costs of any Superfund site to which they had shipped their recycled raw materials, whether or not these raw materials had caused any pollution (which they hadn't). Thus, iron made from recycled scrap metal, for example, was deemed hazardous waste if it was sent to a plant that later became a Superfund site. Ironically, iron ore,

---

[9] This section is based on Diermeier et al. (2017).

its substantially identical virgin counterpart, was not deemed hazardous under the law. Therefore, virgin materials suppliers were exempt from any Superfund cleanup bills.

The judge's ruling plunged the recycling industry into an existential crisis. Other judges were sure to follow the same interpretation, landing the recycling industry with enormous bills. Most scrap recyclers were family businesses with less than forty employees, and they would surely go bankrupt. This prospect was ironic because the environmental movement that spearheaded the Superfund legislation actually supported recycling.

ISRI's director sprang into action. He decided that the only viable option was to amend the Superfund legislative language to clarify that recycled materials were different from waste, so recyclers shouldn't be subject to the same regulations as polluters. The strategy to amend, but not repeal Superfund legislation was controversial because, while it allowed the recyclers to cooperate with environmental activists, it put the recyclers at odds with the large section of American industry which, at the time, hoped to repeal the Superfund program entirely. With the help of lobbyists and sympathetic legislators, ISRI was able to add the necessary amendment to eight bills over the space of eight years. The first seven bills died in committee, meaning that they were never put to a vote, and so were extinguished at the end of each two-year congressional cycle. With each failure, the financial plight of the recyclers became more dire.

Eventually, the eighth bill was successful. What made the difference was direct lobbying by the recyclers' CEOs. After seven failures in seven years, ISRI developed a "fly-in" program whereby the CEOs of many recycling businesses flew into Washington, DC, on the same day and met with their respective representatives. During these meetings, the CEOs were trained to repeat the same simple message: "Scrap is not waste." The repetition of this mantra, and the fact that the CEOs had showed up to give the message in person, finally moved the legislators to pass the bill that saved the recycling industry.

The new law was titled the Superfund Recycling Equity Act. It clarified that recycled materials should be treated differently from hazardous waste. It also provided for all the Superfund fines that had been paid, to be refunded to the recyclers who had paid them. So the recycler's saga had a happy ending.

Learning Points   This case illustrates that adverse regulation can kill an entire industry, especially if the industry is made up of small businesses that, individually, have little influence with the legislature. In the case of the recyclers, a trade association sprang into action and created a coalition that, ultimately, was successful. A second learning point is that suppliers of virgin raw materials were exempt from the Superfund law and, therefore, uninterested in helping the recycling industry. This meant that virgin materials suppliers would not be a motivated coalition partner for the recyclers. Chapter 5 discusses coalition formation.

2.3 FILM CENSORSHIP

In 1896, Thomas Edison introduced a technology that allowed films to be shown on screen rather than, as before, being viewed through a peephole. One of the first films to be shown on screen was a twenty-second film called *The Kiss*, where a man is shown repeatedly kissing a woman. *The Kiss* was a sensation. It was shown all across the country wherever the new screen projection technology was available. In its Atlanta, GA, premiere on November 18, 1896, *The Atlanta Constitution* reports that the film "took the house by storm and had to be repeated several times."[10]

As film technology progressed, demand for risqué content increased. The industry began producing movies involving seduction, crime, sex, and infidelity. These movies were shown in Nickelodeons: crude, ill-ventilated theaters with hard wooden seats where the price of admission was a nickel. The movie industry soon acquired an unsavory reputation. Critics denounced the industry as morally objectionable and as the cause of social unrest and criminal behavior. Some called for censorship.

Censors quickly emerged at the state and local levels. In 1907, the city of Chicago enacted one of the first film censorship laws in America. It was followed by similar laws in many cities and states across the United States. Soon, there were loud calls for federal regulation of the film industry. Three separate congressional bills were introduced to establish a Federal Censorship Commission, but none passed. In 1915, the Supreme Court ruled that movies were not protected by the First Amendment. This ruling gave state and local censors legal protection – and a green light.

Censors became increasingly bold. They would arbitrarily cut scenes from, or entirely reject, movies. In 1917, the Chicago censor rejected a patriotic movie about the American Revolution because it

---

[10] Quoted from Dengler (1979) p. 270.

contained matters offensive to Great Britain, and an anti-German war movie because it would offend German–American citizens.[11]

The impulse toward censorship increased even further when talking movies entered the scene. Father Daniel Lord, a Catholic priest with a powerful political following, was a vocal proponent of censorship. In his words: "Silent smut had been bad, vocal smut cried to the censors for vengeance."

According to Black (1989), Father Lord believed that:

[The movies'] universal popularity, cutting across social, political, and economic classes and penetrating communities from the most sophisticated to the most remote, meant that filmmakers could not be permitted the same freedom of expression allowed to producers of legitimate theater, authors of books, or even editors of newspapers. Movies had to be more restricted, Lord believed, because they were persuasively and indiscriminately seductive.[12]

The argument for censorship was paternalistic and powerful. In a 1926 congressional hearing devoted to the question of establishing federal censorship on the industry, a religious leader called the industry "a threat to world civilization."[13]

By the early 1930s, one-third of American film audiences resided in areas controlled by state or municipal movie censors. The arbitrary and fragmented nature of regulation was a big problem for the industry: The industry was effectively held up by local regulatory boards, and movie producers had lost artistic control over their product.

Faced with clumsy government regulation and activism in the public arena, the movie industry chose to self-regulate. The big five Hollywood studios – Warner Bros, Paramount, RKO, MGM, and Fox Film – formed a trade association: the Motion Picture Producers and Distributors of America (MPPDA). The purpose of the trade association was to prevent federal censorship and roll back local censorship. Its president, Will Hays, asked Father Lord to write a code of conduct for the industry. Thus, in 1930, the *Code to Govern the Making of Motion Pictures* was created. This document, informally referred to as "Hays Code," contains a list of specific "Don'ts and Be Carefuls." Among the "Don'ts" were:

- Profanities and vulgar language
- Nudity
- Drug trafficking

[11] Benzkofer (2015).
[12] Black (1989), pp. 171–172.
[13] Black (1989), p. 170.

- Scenes of actual childbirth
- Ridicule of the clergy
- Willful offense to any nation, race or creed
- Surgical operations
- Excessive or lustful kissing.

The Hays Code was enforced by the industry itself. By 1934, movies without MPPDA certificate couldn't be shown in any theater owned by a major studio, or distributed by any MPPDA member. The Hays Code had teeth: In 1946, the famous director Alfred Hitchcock wanted to feature a long kissing scene in the movie *Notorious*, but he was forced to break up the shot into a series of separate less-than-three-second kisses so as to comply with the Hays Code's prohibition against "lustful kissing."

The Hays Code was so effective in curbing explicit content that federal censorship was never enacted, and local censorship boards stopped interfering with movies. Thus, by self-regulating, the movie industry was able to regain artistic control over its product.

Learning Points The Hays code was a form of self-regulation created by the industry to preempt and replace clumsy and fragmented governmental regulation. The Hays Code was strict: it did not mean absence of all regulations. Rather, it meant efficient regulation because it gave the industry certainty and uniformity of regulation. Are all industries able to preempt clumsy government regulation by replicating what the movie industry did? This question is addressed in Section 9.1.

2.4 STUDENT DEBT RELIEF

The CEOs of the largest US financial firms shifted uncomfortably in their seats. Much to their chagrin, they had been rounded up in a Capitol Hill room to answer unfriendly questions from legislators. The event had been arranged by the House Financial Services Committee to embarrass the CEOs in front of the media. The Fox Business Network was broadcasting the event live with the chyron "Banks Grilled on the Hill." The Committee Chairwoman fired off a question:

"Last year, one million student loan borrowers defaulted, which is on top of the one million borrowers who defaulted the year before. What are you guys doing to help us with this student loan debt? Who would like to answer first? Mr. Monahan, big bank.

"We stopped making student loans in 2007 or so.

"Oh, so you don't do it anymore. Mr. Corbat?

"We exited student lending in 2009.

"Mr. Dimon?

"When the government took over student lending in 2010 or so, we stopped doing all student lending."

These were perfect answers from the point of view of Brian Monahan (CEO, Bank of America), Michael Corbat (CEO, Citigroup), and Jamie Dimon (CEO, JPMorgan Chase). They had had the foresight to exit the student loan market several years before, around the 2008 financial crisis. Their foresight was rewarded years later, during this exchange on Capitol Hill.

Exiting the large and growing student-debt market must not have been an easy call. Before 2008, banks originated most student loans and held about half of all student debt.[14] Market size was already very significant in 2008, with student debt as high as $671 billion.[15] Afterward, market size would continue to grow rapidly, achieving $1.5 trillion in 2021.

And yet, the decision to exit this lucrative market was likely a good one. The student debt issue was a political powder keg. First, a lot of voters were on the hook: by 2021, 30 percent of all adults had incurred some student debt. The median debtor owed more than $20,000.[16] Therefore current debtors, and their families and friends, represented a powerful constituency for extracting some sort of relief or forgiveness from the debt holders.

Had the big banks not exited the student loan market, it is likely that elected officials would have pressured them to give borrowers relief. In 2017, for example, the loan servicing company Navient was sued by thirty-nine US states for predatory lending. It ended up settling for $1.85 billion without admitting fault. While the company was, unsurprisingly, portrayed negatively in the media, the resonance of this lawsuit was limited – the *New York Times*, for example, wrote only one article regarding the settlement.[17] This was the case, likely, because Navient was not a household name.[18] Had any of the big banks been the target of this lawsuit instead of Navient, the publicity surrounding the lawsuit would have been larger and the reputational harm would have been worse.

---

[14] Shohov (2004), p. 107.
[15] Berman (2018).
[16] Board of Governors (2021).
[17] Cowley and Siegel Bernand (2022).
[18] Navient was spun off by the Student Loan Marketing Association (Sallie Mae) in 2014 and, at its peak, serviced $300 billion in student loans.

Learning Point SBM is useful for forecasting changes in an industry's regulatory environment. In Section 5.3, I will use the tools provided in this book to show that the beyond-market fundamentals were all wrong for the big banks in the student loan market. Exiting this lucrative market was a hard call but, in hindsight, it was a good call, and a testament to the predictive power of SBM.

2.5 JUUL

JUUL Labs Inc. was an e-cigarette company based in the United States. The company was founded in 2007 under a different name, with the goal of producing vaporizers. Its most successful product, JUUL, was developed in 2015: It was a single-use nicotine vaporizer with an exceptionally high nicotine concentration. JUUL was available in fruit flavors including mango, apple, and berries. Its appearance resembled a pen drive.

E-cigarettes were a controversial product right from the start. To traditional cigarette smokers, they offered a much healthier nicotine-delivering mechanism than inhaling burned tobacco. To nonsmokers, however, they represented a gateway to nicotine addiction.

Many in the public health community were suspicious of e-cigarettes. They were concerned that nonsmokers, and youth in particular, could become addicted to nicotine by inhaling fruit-flavored vapors. They were especially concerned about JUUL products because they were small, sleek, and could easily be concealed by high school students because they resembled pen drives.

Sales of JUUL exploded. By 2018, JUUL had captured 70 percent share of the fast-growing US e-cigarette market.[19] This success was driven by a shrewd marketing campaign that made use of social media and, many thought, was targeted at a young audience. In fact, the concerns about youth use proved well-founded: By 2019, 27 percent of US high school students were vaping regularly.[20] In addition, a vibrant gray market developed for e-liquids, including cannabis-based ones. These liquids were marketed by fly-by-night businesses, and their pharmacological content was opaque at best.

In December 2018 the company, now renamed after its blockbuster product JUUL, sold 35 percent of its shares to Altria (previously known as Philip Morris Companies, Inc.) at an eye-popping valuation of $38 billion for the entire company. Initially, Altria's shares were nonvoting;

---

[19] TobaccoTactics (2022).
[20] FDA News Release (2019).

but they were soon converted to voting shares, giving Altria control over JUUL's operations. Soon, JUUL's product line was fully integrated with Altria's.[21] In an article titled "The Billion Dollar Startup Club," the *Wall Street Journal* ranked JUUL the fourth most valuable startup in the world based on its February 2019 valuation.[22]

Not everyone was happy with the acquisition, however. Matthew L. Myers, president of the Campaign for Tobacco-Free Kids, said sarcastically:

The Marlboro man rode into Juul and now wants us to trust them.[23]

Ironically, Altria's acquisition marked the beginning of the decline for JUUL. The director of the US Food and Drug Administration (FDA) had initially taken at face value JUUL's stated intentions to suppress teen uptake. However, he felt betrayed by Altria's acquisition. In February 2019, the FDA director tweeted that vaping among teens had increased by 78 percent year-over-year and declared ominously: "Manufacturers and management are accountable for the youth epidemic."[24]

In September 2019, things got worse. An epidemic of lung disease connected with vaping broke out. Six people had died, and medical experts were racing to pinpoint the causes.[25] Eventually, the deaths would be linked to dangerous ingredients in cannabis e-liquids produced by fly-by-night sellers. In the meantime, however, the FDA announced that it would pull all flavored e-cigarettes off the market until further review.[26]

At the time of this writing, the FDA has not yet allowed flavored e-cigarettes back on the market. Instead, in 2020, it issued stringent new regulations concerning the manufacturing, importation, and resale of e-cigarettes and e-liquids. For good measure, the new regulations increased the legal smoking age, including vaping, from 18 to 21 years.[27] Under the new regulations, vape shops that mixed or prepared e-liquids would now be considered manufacturers. The regulatory effort succeeded in curbing youth vaping. In 2021, only 11.3 percent of high school students were using e-cigarettes, less than half the level reached in 2019.[28]

---

[21] TobaccoTactics (2022).
[22] Austin et al. (2019).
[23] Kaplan (2021).
[24] Brodwin (2019).
[25] LaVito (2019a).
[26] LaVito (2019b).
[27] FDA (2020).
[28] Park-Lee et al. (2021).

However, adult vaping also decreased from 8 percent in 2019 to 6 percent in 2021.[29] To the extent that this drop in adult vaping portended a corresponding increase in cigarette smoking, it could be viewed as a cause for concern. In 2021, one out of seven US adults was a smoker, and 480,000 Americans died every year as a result of smoking – a death toll comparable to COVID.[30] In a scientific article, Kenneth Warner, dean emeritus and the Avedis Donabedian Distinguished University Professor Emeritus at the University of Michigan's School of Public Health, stated that:

Multiple types of evidence, identified in our article, demonstrate that vaping can increase smoking cessation. The highly respected Cochrane Review has concluded that it is likely that vaping is more effective than FDA-approved nicotine replacement products like gum and patches. The CDC has also found that more smokers use e-cigarettes than other aids in attempts to quit smoking—and with a higher self-reported success rate. Still, the public is largely unaware of the potential vaping has to aid in smoking cessation.[31]

In September 2021 the FDA formally approved Vuse, a JUUL competitor, for marketing – but not JUUL. Meanwhile, JUUL's market share had shrunk to 42 percent, down from 70 percent in 2018. Its valuation, according to Altria, had been marked down to $5 billion, less than one-seventh of its 2018 level. An effort to expand internationally had fizzled, and the workforce had been cut by three quarters.[32] The company was in real trouble. The *New York Times* summarized JUUL's perilous plight with this title:

Juul Is Fighting to Keep Its E-Cigarettes on the U.S. Market.[33]

Learning Points This case represents a failure to self-regulate on the part of the vaping industry. The industry would probably have been better off by self-regulating than by being harshly regulated by the government. Self-regulation is discussed in Section 9.1.

2.6 "A WORLD WITHOUT FREE KNOWLEDGE"

Anyone who tried to access Wikipedia or Google on January 18, 2012, would have seen the unusual landing pages shown in Figures 2.1 and 2.2.

[29] Cf. Gallup (2022) and Hrynovski and Brenan (2022).
[30] Balfour et al. (2021), p. 1667.
[31] Michigan News (2021).
[32] Kaplan (2021).
[33] Kaplan (2021).

FIGURE 2.1 Wikipedia landing page on January 18, 2012.

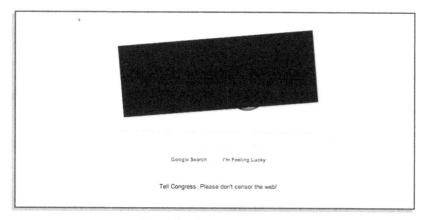

FIGURE 2.2 Google landing page on January 18, 2012.

These pages represented the two websites' public protest against two related bills being discussed in Congress: the Stop Online Piracy Act (SOPA, in the House) and the PROTECT IP Act (PIPA, in the Senate). These two bills were intended to discourage online trafficking in copyrighted and counterfeit goods. So-called "torrent" websites, in particular, were infringing on US intellectual property by allowing anyone to download copyrighted movies, TV shows, and video games. Torrent websites were often based in locations not subject to US jurisdiction, so SOPA and PIPA sought to shut them down by imposing criminal penalties on advertising networks such as Google Ads, and financial institutions such as credit card networks, that did business with the infringing websites.

Moreover, search engines would be forbidden from linking to the infringing websites, and Internet service providers would be required to block access to the websites. Violators could be subject to a penalty of five years in jail. The same severe treatment would also apply to websites that sold counterfeit drugs. This last provision was favored by the US pharmaceutical industry.

The supporters of SOPA and PIPA were a *Who's Who* of America's business elite, including the Motion Picture Association of America (MPAA), media companies such as the American Broadcasting Corporation (ABC), the Columbia Broadcasting System (CBS), Disney, the Recording Industry Association of America, the Entertainment Software Association, Nike, Sony, Comcast, VISA, and the entire pharmaceutical industry. Among SOPA and PIPA's opponents: Wikipedia, Facebook, Google, and Amazon. Although some of the opponents were already very large companies back in 2012, at that time their combined size was not as large as the coalition of SOPA/PIPA's supporters. Also, they employed far fewer Americans, and their lobbying power was much smaller back then.

Early on, the SOPA and PIPA bills were uncontroversial with most members of Congress: American industry supported the bills, and the US economy was highly IP-reliant. Therefore, the Senate Judiciary Committee voted unanimously in favor of PIPA. However, the January 18 "blackout pages" by Wiki and Google changed the equation. The blackout pages were seen by many millions of Americans and were widely reported on by the global media. On that day, fourteen million people in the United States alone, ten million of whom were voters, reached out to lawmakers to voice their disapproval of the bills.[34]

Lawmakers quickly took notice: According to Constine (2012), their U-turn was instantaneous:

At the beginning of January 18th, there were 80 members of congress who supported the legislation, and 31 opponents. Now [the next day], just 63 support SOPA-PIPA, and opposition has surged to 122.

Senator Marco Rubio of Florida, which is home to a large Disney theme park, was an early supporter of PIPA. He summarized the feelings of many of his colleagues in this way:

Earlier this year, this bill passed the Senate Judiciary Committee unanimously and without controversy. Since then, we've heard legitimate concerns about the impact the bill could have on access to the Internet and about a potentially unreasonable

---

[34] Weisman (2012).

expansion of the federal government's power to impact the Internet. Congress should listen and avoid rushing through a bill that could have many unintended consequences. Therefore, I have decided to withdraw my support for the Protect IP Act.[35]

SOPA and PIPA were dead in the water. The bills were dropped, never to be taken up again by Congress.

Learning Points This was a titanic battle. Both sides had the ability to mobilize public opinion: one side via mass media, the other via the Internet. What made the difference was the ability to shape the narrative in the court of public opinion. This issue will be discussed in Section 6.6.

2.7 PINK VIAGRA

An attractive female model lay on a bed, speaking directly to the camera: "What the f**k?? Are we really so far behind that we don't think women have the right to sexual desire?"

This scene was part of a YouTube video created by Sprout Pharmaceutical, the maker of the drug Flibanserin. The video, which went viral, promoted Flibanserin under the brand name Addyi. Addyi was the first medication that addressed a disease called hypoactive sexual desire disorder (HSDD). According to the medication's website:

ADDYI is a prescription medicine used to treat hypoactive (low) sexual desire disorder (HSDD) in women who have not gone through menopause, who have not had problems with low sexual desire in the past, and who have low sexual desire no matter the type of sexual activity, the situation, or the sexual partner. Women with HSDD have low sexual desire that is troubling to them.[36]

Like some anxiolytics and antidepressants, Flibanserin worked through the brain's serotonin receptors, which are involved in impulse control. For the treatment to have any effect, Flibanserin had to be taken daily for a prolonged period – several months.

The drug had a troubled history with the US FDA. The first time Flibanserin was submitted to the FDA for approval, it was rejected unanimously on the grounds that the drug did not show statistically significant improvements in sexual desire, but it had significant side effects. The side effects included dizziness, and blood pressure drop when taken in conjunction with alcohol. After this disappointing outcome Boehringer,

---

[35] Sanchez (2012).
[36] https://addyi.com/, accessed January 29, 2022.

the drug's manufacturer, gave up and sold the patent to Sprout Pharmaceutical, a small company based in Raleigh, NC. Sprout resubmitted the application to the FDA, and was denied again.

Then, Sprout hired a public relations consultant. The consultant created a grassroots coalition which it named *Even the Score*. The name reflected the coalition's shared view that it was unfair that men had many drugs available for treating low sexual desire, including Viagra, but women had none.[37] Many reputable women organizations joined the coalition, including the National Organization for Women, the Society for Women's Health Research, the International Society for the Study of Women's Sexual Health, Black Women's Health Imperative, and Jewish Women International.

Even the Score put together a public opinion campaign it named "26-0," highlighting the fact that, allegedly, men had twenty-six drugs available to improve their libido, including Viagra, whereas women had none. The campaign created a website with tabs that allowed viewers to "Contact Congress," "Sign the petition," "Share your story," and "Join the movement." The @eventhescore Twitter handle featured a steady flow of supporting tweets, ostensibly from the public.

The *Even the Score* coalition persuaded eleven members of Congress to write to the FDA commissioner to encourage her to approve the drug. The letter mentioned concerns about gender disparities in the approval of treatments for sexual dysfunction. Catchy social media content, including the video mentioned at the top of this section, was a key part of the campaign. A supportive legacy media industry picked up on the campaign and framed it within a gender equity narrative. The new drug soon acquired the moniker "Pink Viagra."

Some women organizations, however, were disturbed by Sprout's public opinion campaign. They noted the drug's high risk-to-benefit ratio, and believed that "Pink Viagra" might even be harmful. They denounced the media campaign as instrumental and tried to push back in the court of public opinion. However, their voices were not amplified by the media, and their counternarrative never became salient enough to make a difference.[38]

---

[37] The analogy between Flibanserin and Viagra was not entirely apt. Viagra and other drugs for men did not treat low libido, but, rather, they improved blood flow to the key body organ. Also, they were taken on an "as needed" basis. Flibanserin, in contrast, was analogous to an antidepressant, and it needed to be taken every day for a month before expecting it to have an effect.

[38] Block and Canner (2016).

Sprout re-submitted the drug for FDA approval. As the media was reporting on Addyi's potential benefits, the FDA was holding patient-focused meetings. Sprout flew in supportive patients to these meetings, who made the case that approving Addyi would represent a step in redressing the FDA's past gender inequities. At one of these meetings, the government-relations director for the National Organization for Women said, to loud applause: "It's time to start believing what women say about their sex lives."[39]

The third time was the charm: the FDA approved the drug with a panel recommendation of 18–6. Two days later Sprout Pharmaceutical, a company with just thirty-four employees, sold Addyi to the Canadian pharmaceutical giant Valeant for $1 billion.

Learning Points This case illustrates that regulators (in this case, the FDA) are vulnerable when their expertise is questioned. Sprout's strategy leveraged this vulnerability by implying that the FDA did not operate according to impartial scientific standards, but, rather, it was subject to gender bias. The particular bias seemed plausible, so the threat to the FDA's reputation seemed real. This threat caused the FDA to crumble under the pressure. The strategy of questioning the regulators' expertise is discussed in Section 8.

---

[39] Block and Canner (2016).

3

How Do the Rules of the Competitive Game Change?

The common feature across the illustrative examples in Chapter 2 is that the firm's ability to preserve or create value hinges on its ability to influence the rules of the competitive game. But who makes – and can change – the rules of the game?

In every democratic country, the political system has *institutions* that make and change laws and regulations. This chapter sketches out, in broad strokes, how these institutions work. In a sense, this chapter is standard civics, except that an unconventional viewpoint is adopted: that of business instead of citizens. This chapter, therefore, may be thought of as "civics from a business perspective."

3.1 THE RULE MAKERS: ELECTED OFFICIALS AND REGULATORS

The rule makers – the people who make laws and regulations – fall into two categories: elected officials and regulators.

Elected Officials   Elected officials make laws and, in the case of elective executive positions (such as the US president), execute them.

Definition 4 (Elected Officials)   *Elected officials are government officials who are elected by the public, as opposed to appointed by another official. Legislators (e.g., a US senator) and some executive positions (such as the US president or a state governor) are elected officials. Elected officials are motivated by the prospect of reelection or election to higher office.*

Democracies provide for citizens to elect politicians so that the politicians may represent their constituents' preferences over public policies.

Therefore, the role of elected officials is to aggregate their constituents' diverse preferences and champion them. Politicians are very responsive to what their constituents want. Chapter 4 deals with elected officials.

Need for Technical Expertise   In order to carry out their duties, elected officials must leverage technical knowledge possessed by others. For example, the US president and other executive officers must necessarily rely on administrators – for instance, employees of the Department of Justice – to execute their mandate. These administrators have the time and the technical expertise to ensure that the laws of the US are faithfully executed.

Legislators, too, must avail themselves of considerable technical knowledge in order to make laws. Consider, for example, the US Noise Control Act. As the name suggests, this law was passed to control environmental noise. The aim of this law was expressed in a single sentence on page 1 of the act: "[T]o promote an environment for all Americans free from noise that jeopardizes their health or welfare."[1]

This single sentence, despite being simple and noncontroversial, required twenty additional pages of legislation to spell out its meaning in a way that made it implementable by the administration, the courts, and the private sector. Indeed, the rest of the Noise Control Act included two pages of definitions that made precise the language contained in the first page; nine more pages of instructions for federal agencies (i.e., the regulators) about what they needed to do after the Act was approved; and, finally, nine additional pages specifying who had standing to sue under the Act, the actions that private manufacturers (of planes, cars, motorcycles, etc.) must take, and so on.

Who wrote these twenty pages? Most legislators probably didn't understand the technicalities that make up pages 2–20 of the act. These legislators probably only read page 1 and then voted based on their party's advice. Some legislators might have read all twenty pages, and perhaps even contributed a few lines at their constituents' behest: The airline industry, for example, would likely have had an interest in this law due to the concerns raised by engine noise around airports and over land. But, mostly, the technical language would have been drafted by regulators, likely with heavy input from the industry.

---

[1]   42 U.S. Code § 4901, Sec. 2b, www.law.cornell.edu/uscode/text/42/4901.

In sum, the Noise Control Act contained a short nontechnical prescription ("promote an environment free from noise"), and then twenty pages of technical language written by technical experts. True, the power to vote on and approve the entire twenty pages rested with legislators; but legislators couldn't have written the law without technical assistance. To get a sense of the social cost of getting the technical language wrong, refer back to the Recyclers' case in Section 2.2: There, a single mistaken reference to "waste" in the language of the Superfund law triggered an existential crisis for an entire industry that took many years to resolve. The general lesson is that there is a division of labor: Elected officials have the formal power to pass laws but, to write laws that are practically implementable, they need to rely on technical experts.

Regulators Regulators are unelected technical experts. The top regulators are appointed by elected officials (they are referred to as "political appointees"), and they are often replaced when the government changes. The lower-level regulators are generally hired for life: These are the career bureaucrats in the governmental departments or ministries. The regulators' function is to inject technical knowledge into the language of the laws, to write implementing regulations that make sense, and to ensure that the laws are being followed.

Definition 5 (Regulators) *Regulators are unelected technical experts whose function is to inject technical knowledge into the language of the laws, to write implementing regulations, and to monitor that the laws are being followed.*

To appreciate the difference between what regulators and legislators do, consider what happened *after* the Noise Control Act became law. At that moment, the regulators started working on the Act's *implementation*. A host of technical choices needed to be made regarding the permissible noise level for aircraft and motorcycles, how these noise levels would be measured, and so on. Some of these regulations would have been specifically foreshadowed in the language of the Noise Control Act; others would have been initiated by the regulators themselves. On average in the United States, less than half of the rules issued by regulators are specifically mandated by congressional statute.[2]

To get a sense of the granularity of the implementing regulations, point your browser to www.ecfr.gov and type "noise control act" in the search

---

[2] See Yackee (2019), p. 43.

box. The search returns all the technical choices that were made by regulators in connection with the Act and that, collectively, represent the Act's *implementing regulations*.

Regulatory Discretion   As this example suggests, regulators have a lot of discretion when writing implementing regulations. To keep regulators accountable, the law requires them to alert the general public before issuing a new regulation, to share the text of the proposed regulation, and to allow anyone to send in comments. Although these comments are not binding for the regulator, nevertheless this requirement helps keep the regulator accountable to knowledgeable members of the public, including industry experts.

Other Regulatory Functions   After a law is passed and its implementing regulations are written, regulators typically continue to be involved. They may play a big role in the *administration* of a law, which involves organizing and recording business compliance with the law. Finally, regulators sometimes have quasi-judicial *enforcement* power to punish violators.

The Hidden Power of Regulators   Most scholars agree that regulators play an increasingly significant role in shaping today's economy, compared with legislators. In the words of a leading scholar: "Government regulations set the standards for almost every aspect of American life.... Given the pervasiveness of rulemaking, US public policymaking may be better conceived of as chiefly regulatory, rather than chiefly legislative."[3]

Learning Points   Elected officials are accountable to voters. They are not technical experts. Downstream of them are regulators, technical experts that are not elected but, rather, appointed. In theory, elected officials have all the power. In practice, regulators have a lot of hidden power.

3.2 WHERE DOES BUSINESS FIT IN?

Formally, business has very little input in the making of the rules: The system is designed to keep the rule makers, that is, elected officials and regulators, accountable to voters, not corporations. Informally, however, the business sector as a whole is influential with the rule makers because it has much to offer them.

Sources of Influence   What assets does the business sector have that makes it influential with the rule makers? What can a business offer the

3 Yackee (2019), p. 39.

rule makers? To elected officials, the business sector can offer job creation and support in forming coalitions. New jobs are of paramount importance for any elected official because, in the next election, the official will want to claim that s/he has "created jobs" for voters. In addition, a business interest can act as a policy entrepreneur and help an elected official form a coalition of interest groups that supports the politician's agenda. The coalition formation activity may include a public opinion strategy. More on this topic in Section 4.3.

To regulators, a business can offer compliance and information. When a regulator looks at a business that s/he oversees, s/he sees a source of risk and information. The risk is that something might go wrong: A crisis in the business itself or, worse, in the entire industry. Crises are what regulators fear most because they reflect badly on their competence. If a business complies with regulations, the probability of a crisis in that business is reduced, so the regulators feel that the business is behaving cooperatively. Moreover, the business may possess information that, if shared with the regulator in a timely fashion, could help the regulator prevent an industry-level crisis.

Because the business sector as a whole has much to offer the rule makers, industries or even individual businesses can be influential with elected officials and regulators. Of course, not every business is expected to be equally influential: Influence is proportional to the size of the business (with elected officials) and to the information it possesses (with regulators).

Learning Points   The business sector as a whole has much to offer to the rule makers: jobs, resources for coalition formation, and information. Therefore, the business sector can be influential with elected officials and regulators, even though neither is formally accountable to industry.

3.3 FORMS OF BUSINESS ADVOCACY

In the United States, there are three channels through which industries or individual businesses can advocate for a preferred policy agenda: They can contribute money to a legislator's political campaign, help create a coalition that supports the legislator's policy goals, and provide persuasive information to legislators and regulators. To operate within these advocacy channels, businesses sometimes rely on government relations experts and lobbyists.

Many people think that the main channel of business influence with government officials is campaign contributions or, worse, corrupt favors.

In the United States, this is largely untrue.[4] As I discuss more extensively in Section 4.3, campaign contributions represent only a small fraction of what the business sector spends on influence activities. Most of the money is spent on lobbying, which means that firms pay someone – a lawyer, or a former elected official – to make arguments regarding jobs, technology, and economic growth, in a way that the rule makers find persuasive. This activity is what political scientists call "informational lobbying." In addition, a lobbyist may help create a coalition of interests that supports the shared goals that its client and selected elected officials have in common. The general consensus among political scientists is that, in today's United States, most of the firm's influence over the political process takes place not through campaign contributions but, rather, through informational lobbying and, in addition, through the deployment of private resources that empower government officials to pursue their own public policy agendas.

Because, in the United States, most of the influence of business on government does not arise from a corrupt exchange of money or favors for policies but, rather, from information provision and coalition formation, the second and third advocacy channels are the main focus of this book, not the first.

Learning Points In today's United States, most of the business sector's influence over the political process takes place through information provision and coalition formation. The influence of business on government does not, in the main, come from a corrupt exchange of money or favors for policies.

3.4 DIFFERENTIAL OPENNESS TO BUSINESS ADVOCACY ACROSS POLITICAL SYSTEMS

For the business sector to be able to advocate with the rule makers, access is critical. Not all political systems – federal, states, and cities – are equally open to business advocacy. True, the largest firms enjoy good access in all political systems. However, this is not necessarily the case for the rest of the firms. How easy is it for a "regular" business to make its case with the rule makers? This depends on two specific characteristics of a political system: whether the political system is pluralist or corporatist,

---

[4] Outside the United States, the picture is different. Cash payments to politicians or parties are a factor in many countries, though they are increasingly uncommon in advanced countries.

and whether it is federal or centralized. As a point of reference, the US federal government is pluralist and federal. US state governments need not be pluralist and, depending on the issue, regulatory powers may or may not be decentralized: For example, the regulation of taxicabs tends to be decentralized because it is delegated to substate jurisdictions such as cities.

Pluralism versus Corporatism   Democratic political systems lie somewhere on a continuum between two extremes. At one extreme are pluralistic systems, where direct access is relatively easy even for moderately sized firms. At the other extreme are corporatist systems, where moderately sized firms find it difficult to gain direct access.

Definition 6 (Pluralism)   *A pluralistic political system is one where individual firms enjoy unmediated, relatively easy, and transparent access to legislators and regulators, and a well-regulated lobbying industry is available to help connect a firm with legislators and regulators.*

To illustrate the notion of pluralism, I will rely on cross-country comparisons, even though this book is primarily concerned with the United States. Among the world's countries, the United States is the most pluralistic one – but not the only pluralistic one. Jahn (2016) provides an index that locates forty-two industrialized countries on the pluralist-corporatist spectrum. Among all the countries ranked by this index, the United States is the most pluralistic one, followed by Canada and the UK. The least pluralistic country is Austria. The opposite of pluralism is corporatism.

Definition 7 (Corporatism)   *A corporatist political system is one where direct access to legislators and regulators is difficult for most individual firms except the largest ones, access is controlled by monopolistic industry associations, and lobbying is opaque and unregulated.*

Continental European countries tend to be relatively corporatist. According to the above-mentioned index, Austria is the most corporatist country in the sample, while France and Portugal are in the middle of the ranking. Next, I briefly describe how business advocacy takes place in pluralistic and corporatist systems.

Structure of Pluralistic Systems, Such as the United States   The United States is probably the country whose political system is most open to business advocacy by both large and small firms. One reason is that there is no shortage of advocacy targets: among them, no less than 535 members of Congress. As a consequence, access in the United States is relatively unrestricted: Even relatively small businesses can contact their representative's office, make an appointment, and make their case with the representative – or at least with a legislative assistant. Also very important, each of the 535 member of Congress has meaningful agency: S/he can, for example, introduce a bill to Congress and attempt to put together a coalition to push the bill forward.[5] This combination of target-richness and diffuse agency is peculiar to the US political system.

A third defining feature of the US system is a competitive and professional lobbying industry. For a relatively small amount of money, a lobbyist or government relations professional can take care of the logistics of a meeting with a legislator and assist with the crafting and implementation of an advocacy strategy. These three features imply that direct access is relatively easy even for moderately sized firms.

Structure of Corporatist Systems   In corporatist political systems, direct access to the political system is difficult except for the largest firms. A first major reason is that advocacy targets are scarce. In corporatist systems, individual lawmakers have little agency and, as a result, are not targeted by their constituents. Party leaders are much more important. The next quote makes this point.

> Voters often do not know their MPs [members of parliament]. Even where they do, in Europe the personal vote is weak compared to the party component. [... G]overnments are created, maintained and brought down by the decisions of party leaders. While MPs are crucial for the implementation of these decisions, they hardly make them in their capacity as deputies.[6]

While this quote refers to Europe, it also applies to other corporatist political systems across the world. In these systems, most legislators have negligible political autonomy: the vast majority of political decisions are made by the party leaders alone.[7] Therefore, most legislators are not

---

[5] Most political systems across the world are different. There, rank-and-file representatives are strictly controlled by their party leaders. The US representatives' comparatively high agency is generally ascribed to the fact that the United States has a "weak party system," meaning that representatives are highly responsive to their constituents. In countries with "strong party systems," representatives are highly responsive to their political party leader.

[6] Müller (2000, p. 311).

[7] These are called "strong party" systems. How can you tell parties strong in a given country? A good indication is that voters vote for the party, not the person. But what makes parties strong in one country and weak in another? An important factor is how much control parties have on the electoral ballot, that is, on who among the party representatives voters are allowed to vote for. When parties control the ballot, they tend to be strong because then the party leader can threaten to "dis-ballot" individual legislators. Wherever, instead, access to the ballot is determined by a primary contest, parties tend to be weaker.

meaningful targets of advocacy: only the party leaders are. But party leaders are few in number – maybe two or three in a given coalition government – so access to them is necessarily scarce.[8]

How, then, is scarce access rationed in corporatist systems? Access to the political system is controlled by monopolistic trade associations. Often, these associations are recognized by law and organized hierarchically. For example, a small industry, say, port marinas, would have its own trade association (association of port marinas) which, in turn, would be a member of a larger umbrella association (say, a marine industry association), which would itself be a member of an apex organization (say, an all-industry confederation). The apex organization collaborates with the government in the writing of laws and regulations. Since these trade associations are dominated by older and larger firms, it is difficult for smaller and younger firms to be heard. In a corporatist system, therefore, the oldest and largest firms are effectively the gatekeepers.

Most countries with corporatist systems have no formal lobbying sector. Instead, what lobbying activity exists outside of trade associations is unregulated and opaque. These features imply that direct access is difficult for moderately-sized firms.

How Business Advocacy Differs between Pluralistic and Corporatist Systems   The difference in the advocacy environment between the United States and Europe is revealed by two metrics. First, party discipline is much higher in Europe: legislators there almost always vote in lockstep with their party. This is not the case in the United States: For example, of all the bills that were signed into law in 2018, nearly 70 percent were cosponsored by at least one Democrat and at least one Republican.[9] More systematic evidence is provided by the Rice index of party voting unity, which measures the degree to which party members vote in lockstep. This index is considerably lower in the United States than in every European country.[10] This difference indicates that ad hoc coalitions, meaning coalitions of representatives who cross party lines in

---

[8] Leaders of parties that are not part of the government are not primary advocacy targets because, by and large, they do not have the power to influence policy.

[9] Quorum (2018).

[10] According to Brady (2014), "In a survey of 16 European countries plus Australia and New Zealand, which includes 90 political parties, the lowest party unity scores were 88.63 for Finland and 93.17 for New Zealand, with the average for all sixteen countries being over 97. In contrast ... over time in the US Congress, the index's high score is 66 and, even when adjusted, is in the 75 range."

order to support a specific piece of legislation, are relatively common in the United States but relatively rare in Europe.

A second revealing metric of the difference between business advocacy in the United States and in Europe, is the number of bills that are introduced but fail. In the United States, so many bills are introduced in Congress that about 95 percent of them are not even voted on, and of the remaining 5 percent, only about half pass.[11] By contrast, a study of legislative productivity in four European countries reveals that, in each country, more than 20 percent of bills that are introduced pass.[12] This means that access to the legislative arena is more restricted in Europe than in the United States.

These large differences in party cohesion and percentage of failed bills are indicative of the vast difference between pluralism and corporatism. In a pluralistic system, SBM is a free-for-all competition between many opposing interests – often, pitting one ad hoc business coalition against another. Small and large business interests are able to introduce many bills because the barriers to business advocacy are low, so business advocacy takes place in the open. In a corporatist system, in contrast, access to the political arena is difficult for most individual firms: Trade associations act as gatekeepers and are dominated by large and established businesses. Fewer bills are introduced, business advocacy is less manifest and takes place in the dark, often before bills are even introduced.

In pluralistic countries there is a professional and competitive lobbying industry. While in the popular imagination lobbyists are associated with corruption, in fact, the existence of a professional and competitive lobbying industry means that access to the political system is relatively open and transparent. By hiring a lobbyist, even relatively small firms can get the opportunity to make their case with government officials. In most countries with corporatist systems, by contrast, the absence of a professional lobbying sector means that the lobbying activity is unregulated and opaque, which puts smaller firms at a disadvantage.

Federal Structure Openness to business advocacy also depends on whether the political system has a federal structure. In federations such as the United States or the European Union, where the constituent jurisdictions have considerable regulatory autonomy, a business may find it more expedient to access the rule makers in a constituent jurisdiction

---

[11] www.govtrack.us/congress/bills/statistics
[12] See Bräuninger and Debus (2009), Figure 1.

rather than the federal rule makers. The next minicase illustrates how the large degree of autonomy enjoyed by US states allowed a single state to create and adopt technology-friendly regulation. In the minicase, cryptocurrency entrepreneurs found that the state of Wyoming was willing to work with them to make its commercial and banking laws crypto-friendly, at a time when the federal government was not willing to engage with the cryptocurrency industry.

Minicase 1: Cryptocurrency regulation in Wyoming

The year was 2017 and Caitlin Long, a wealthy alumna of the University of Wyoming, was seeking to make a donation to her alma mater.[a] She wanted to make the donation in Bitcoin, but Wyoming state law prevented the university from accepting Bitcoin. Long became frustrated.

As luck would have it, Long had been a managing director at Morgan Stanley and was well positioned to change the rules of the game. Long started working with Wyoming legislators to develop new rules for crypto banking. Most other US states would not touch the crypto banking issue because federal banking regulators were hostile to cryptocurrencies, but Wyoming saw an opportunity to innovate. Long was put in charge of the legislative committee tasked with writing new rules for cryptocurrency.

Fast-forward to 2020, Wyoming had new property laws on its books that clarified what it meant to own a digital asset, permitted banks to be custodians of such, and extended bankruptcy laws to digital assets. In September of that year, Wyoming issued the first-in-America crypto bank charter to the cryptocurrency trading company Kraken.[b] At the time of this writing, Wyoming was home to three crypto banks.

[a] This minicase is based on Wilson (2022).
[b] Bank Policy Institute (2020).

Because Wyoming was open to advocacy by small and innovative firms whereas federal regulators were not, it was possible for this state to partner with the industry in building a tech-forward and innovative regulatory regime. There are many other examples where innovative businesses find it easier to work with (or, sometimes, against) smaller government units.

Uber's success in changing the rules of the game, for example, has been due in part to the fact that the rule makers were city regulators, as opposed to state or federal regulators. It is doubtful that Uber could have succeeded if it had to deal with the federal government rather than with city governments.

Learning Points   Different political systems differ in ease of direct access for moderately-sized businesses. Pluralistic systems are the most open to new and small firms: accessing political representatives to make one's case is relatively easy, and lobbyists can facilitate access. In corporatist systems, in contrast, large and established firms enjoy preferential access to government officials. New and small firms find it difficult to make their case directly, as opposed to through monopolistic industry associations. Finally, access opportunities tend to be more available in federal systems than in centralized ones. The US federal system is pluralist and federal and, hence, relatively easy to access even for moderately sized businesses.

3.5 WHAT ABOUT THE COURTS?

Courts can be viewed as a type of regulator, albeit one with especially limited discretion because the courts are supposed to apply the rules mechanically. In reality, courts have some latitude in interpreting regulations and, occasionally, their decisions can change the rules of the game just as much as elected officials or regulators do. Refer, for example, to the judicial decision that gave rise to the Recyclers case (Section 2.2). Yet, this book is largely silent about the role of courts. The reason is that the subject is actually quite rich, but at a level of detail that makes it suitable for legal specialists, not business people. I am not a legal scholar, and this book is addressed to business practitioners, not lawyers.

The one thing I will say is that, as regards SBM, the courts are the refuge of the weak. So, for example, when a small business is predated upon by a larger one, the small business may lack the heft and size to successfully operate in the political or regulatory arena. In this case, the small business' only recourse may be to sue. More generally, when a business lacks influence with elected officials, regulators, and public opinion, its only recourse may be the courts.

Learning Points   When a business lacks influence with elected officials, regulators, or public opinion, and thus cannot operate effectively in the beyond-market arena, its last resort may be the courts. This book will not discuss the court system.

3.6 THE 4IS FRAMEWORK

The previous sections in this chapter have discussed, in turn: the institutions responsible for changing the rules of the competitive game, that is, elected officials and regulators (Section 3.1); how businesses advocate with either elected officials or with regulators (Sections 3.2 and 3.3); and how the business advocacy landscape differs across democratic political systems worldwide (Section 3.4). Next, building on this knowledge, I provide a framework that is intended to orient strategy for any issue arising in the beyond-market arena.

Every SBM issue can be couched into a diagnostic framework called the 4Is. The 4Is framework reveals the fundamental structure of any SBM problem; every SBM analysis must start with the 4Is.[13] Framework 1 lists the constituent elements of the 4Is.

Framework 1: The 4Is

The constituent elements of the 4Is are:

1. **Issue:** This refers to a change in laws or regulations that affects a business or industry.
2. **Institution:** This refers to the elected officials or regulators that have jurisdiction over the Issue.
3. **Interests:** These are the people or organizations who are affected, either positively or negatively, by the Issue.
4. **Information:** This is what the Interests and Institution know, or might be made aware of, regarding the Issue.

Henceforth, for expositional clarity, I will capitalize the first letter of a constituent element of the 4Is when it is worth emphasizing that the word is used in connection with the 4Is. The 4Is framework may be represented in matrix form as shown in Figure 3.1.

How to Fill Out the 4Is Matrix   The 4Is matrix is filled in from top to bottom, and from left to right. The first matrix element is the Issue. The Issue refers to a change in laws or regulations that a business seeks, or seeks to avoid.

When filling out the 4Is matrix, it is best to formulate the Issue as specifically as possible: For example, in the Recyclers case of Section 2.2, it is better to write: "amend, but do not repeal" the Superfund law, as

---

[13] The 4Is framework is due to David Baron of Stanford GSB.

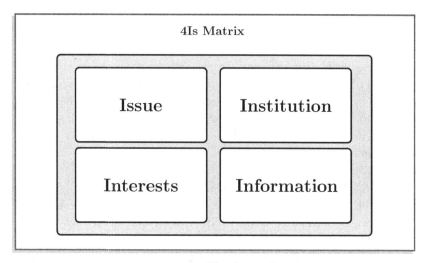

FIGURE 3.1 The 4Is matrix.

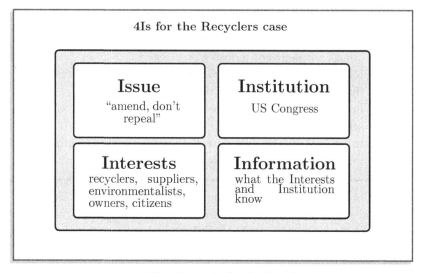

FIGURE 3.2 The 4Is matrix for the Recyclers case.

shown in Figure 3.2, than the less precise formulation "get relief from Superfund lawsuits." The more precise formulation will help pin down the relevant Institution and societal Interests. Indeed, explicit reference to amending a law automatically pins down the legislature as the relevant Institution; and the qualification of "no repeal" clarifies that environmental interests are not necessarily against the Issue, while big industry may well be.

The next matrix element is the Institution. This is, quite simply, either the elected officials or the regulators that have jurisdiction over the Issue. The term jurisdiction refers to the formal authority to make a decision, which is determined by legal rules. For example, in Minicase 1 at page 33, regulators in Wyoming have jurisdiction over the technical implementation of digital bankruptcy law, but not over the writing of such law. Writing a digital bankruptcy law is too large an issue for regulators to have jurisdiction over – they don't have that high level of formal authority. Only the legislature has the legal authority to write a bankruptcy law. The legislature, therefore, is said to have jurisdiction over bankruptcy law.[14] In the Recyclers case, the Institution is the US Congress because the Issue is "amend a law," and only Congress, not any regulator, has the power to do that. Note that, had the Issue not been specified precisely, there could be ambiguity as to which is the relevant Institution.

The Interests, sometimes referred to as interest groups, are people or organizations who are affected, either positively or negatively, by the Issue. In the Recyclers case these include: The recycling businesses, virgin material suppliers, owners of the Superfund sites, environmental activists, and the rest of the American citizens. Note that the 4Is framework does not require one to specify which Interests are in favor or against the Issue.

Often, Interests whose motivation is very low need not be listed in the 4Is framework. Also, Interests that do not have influence with the Institution can be omitted. For example, in the Recyclers case, foreign manufacturers are not listed in the 4Is (see Figure 3.2) because they have very little influence on the Institution, even though they benefit from the recyclers' exported products.

A very important note: the US Congress is not listed among the Interests for two reasons. First, because it is already listed among the Institutions. Second, because members of Congress do not have direct preferences over the Issue: Their actions are guided by a desire to honor the preferences of their constituents, that is, of the voters and businesses located in their district. This is a general principle: In the 4Is framework, Institutions and Interests don't mix. The principle reflects the foundational behavioral assumption in SBM that Institutions have no direct preferences over the Issue over which they have jurisdiction but, rather,

---

[14] Technically, one could argue that the legislature also has jurisdiction over the technical implementation of digital bankruptcy law, and, if it so chooses, it can specify technical parameters. While this is true theoretically, in practice the legislature will not trouble itself with these technical details.

they respond to Interests and Information. A partial exception to this principle is that an Institution may properly be listed among the Interests for Issues over which that Institution has no jurisdiction. For example, the state of Wyoming may well be listed as an Interest on Issues over which the federal government has jurisdiction.

The last matrix entry is the Information. This entry refers to the information that Interests and Institutions have about the Issue. Information can be shared strategically to create coalitions of Interests, as ISRI's director did with the environmentalists. Or, if the Institution is a regulator, information can be shared with the regulator directly. In the Recyclers case, the director of the recyclers' trade association probably had the most accurate and complete information about the Issue. The least informed Interests were undoubtedly the American citizens who, on average, probably knew next to nothing about the recycling industry's perilous plight. The rest of the Interests listed in Figure 3.2 were probably well informed.

Best Practices for Filling Out the 4Is Framework Filling out the 4Is framework is most useful if it is done thoughtfully. Next, I outline some best practices.

First, adopt a minimalistic approach that sharply circumscribes the Issue. This is desirable because it forces the beyond-market strategist to be focused and realistic in defining the strategy's agenda. Unfocused or over-ambitious agendas are flawed and not conducive to SBM success. These flaws are exposed when filling out the Institution entry in the matrix: having to list a proliferation of Institutions, including several regulatory agencies, state and national legislatures, and so on, is a red flag that the Issue is unfocused or overambitious.

Second, make sure that the Institution is either a regulator or a legislator. Sometimes, the process of filling out the 4Is matrix reveals that neither holds the key to success; this is an indication that the problem facing the firm lies outside the field of SBM. If, for example, the critical issue is to regain the trust of customers, or to successfully fight a lawsuit, the tools of SBM may not be helpful.

Third, make sure that the form of business advocacy is appropriate for the Institution. As mentioned in Section 3.2, there are two main forms of business advocacy: coalition formation, and information provision. Speaking very generally, coalition formation is the default form of advocacy when elected officials are the Institution; information provision is the default form of advocacy when regulators are the Institution. This

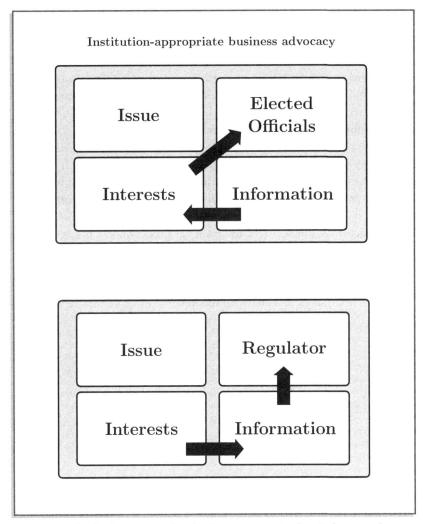

FIGURE 3.3   Institution-appropriate business strategy in the 4Is framework.

general principle is represented visually in Figure 3.3. Panel (a) depicts the principle that, when elected officials are the Institution, information must be targeted to the Interests and aimed at creating coalitions which, in turn, will exert influence with the Institution. Panel (b) depicts the principle that, when regulators are the Institution, Interests should generate information which is then conveyed to the Institution.

Learning Points   Every SBM issue can be couched into the 4Is diagnostic framework. Every SBM analysis must start with the 4Is.

3.7 TAKEAWAYS FROM THIS CHAPTER

All political systems have institutions, that is, elected officials and regulators, that make and change laws and regulations. Elected officials make laws and are motivated by the prospect of reelection or election to higher office. Regulators are unelected technical experts whose function is to inject technical knowledge into the language of the laws, and then to write implementing regulations that make sense.

Formally, business has very little input in the making of rules. Informally, however, the business sector as a whole is influential with the rule makers because it has much to offer them: jobs, coalitions, and information. Therefore, industries or even individual businesses can be influential with elected officials and regulators. In today's United States, most of the business sector's influence over the political process takes place through coalition formation and informational lobbying, not through a corrupt exchange of policies for money or favors.

Every SBM issue can be couched into the 4Is diagnostic framework. Every SBM analysis must start with the 4Is.

4

Elected Officials and Coalitions

The trouble with a politician's life is that somebody is always interrupting it with an election.

Will Rogers
American humorist

This chapter describes who elected officials are, what motivates them, and how corporations advocate with them.

4.1 WHO ARE ELECTED OFFICIALS

Politicians are not like the rest of us. Demographically, that is, elected officials are not representative of the US population. In 2022, members of Congress were more male (72 percent) and more educated (96 percent have a college degree) than the average US population.[1] Personality-wise, politicians are more extroverted, agreeable, and conscientious, than the average American.[2] They are also better-looking.[3] Since politicians are demographically and temperamentally different, should SBM take account of the elected officials' individual characteristics, including their personal views and values?

At the level of analysis of this book, we will not be much concerned with the individual characteristics of elected official. Different from

---

[1] Congressional Research Service (2022).
[2] From a study of US state representatives. Apparently, Republican politicians are more conscientious and less agreeable than Democrat politicians. See Hanania (2017).
[3] Fun fact: Historically, US presidents have been significantly taller than the average adult male. See Persico et al. (2003).

regulators, who are weakly accountable, the elected officials' personal views and values don't majorly affect their political activity because elected officials are strictly accountable to their constituents.[4] Being selected by majority vote ensures that elected officials mostly do what their constituents want them to do. This means that, in the main, the personal characteristics of elected officials are not important from the perspective of SBM: Politically, elected officials channel their median constituent even if they might not look like them, or even feel like them.

Does this mean that the elected officials' individual characteristics, views, and values are totally separate from their political activity? Of course not. Politicians are human after all, so their personal values and beliefs can, occasionally, be reflected in their political activity. For example, a clever study shows that among US legislators with children, those who happen to have more female children are also somewhat more likely to vote liberally on bills concerning women's issues.[5] This evidence suggests that personal experience shapes elected officials' political behavior – but only to some extent.

In sum, the personal characteristics of elected officials are not of great significance in the context of SBM. Their constituents' preferences are the largest determinant of elected officials' political behavior. This, incidentally, is the reason why Institutions are not listed as Interests in the 4Is framework of Section 3.6: The behavior of elected officials reflects their constituents' preferences.

Learning Points Elected officials are strongly incentivized to cater to their median constituent's desires. The individual characteristics of elected officials are mostly unimportant from the perspective of SBM.

4.2 WHAT MOTIVATES ELECTED OFFICIALS

Fear of Losing Losing an election is a traumatic event. Senator Max Cleland, a war hero and triple amputee, described his response to losing an election in this way:

Losing my race for reelection was having a profound effect on me. Another grenade had blown up in my face – this time on the political battlefield rather than the military battlefield. The election was just like the grenade. Over and done in

---

[4] I will spend several pages on the values and beliefs of regulators in Chapter 7.
[5] Washington (2008). Voting liberally means voting in a manner approved by the women rights group NOW.

an instant, with no appeal. No, we can't put your life back together again. No, you can't have your limbs back. No, you can't have your Senate seat back. That life is over now.[6]

While every politician is different – very few, to be sure, have had Senator Cleland's harrowing life experiences – there is no doubt that all politicians fear losing the next election. This fear is the main source of incentives for elected officials.

Radical Uncertainty   Being reelected is not easy. Despite what most people think, at any given moment there is tremendous uncertainty about what voters really want, as opposed to what surveys and polls say they want, and therefore about what an elected officials should do to please their constituents. Therefore, in their pursuit of reelection, politicians operate in an environment of radical uncertainty. Moreover, voters can change their mind: A policy that is popular at time $t - 1$ may not be popular at time t, when the election is held. Finally, politicians can get blamed for many contingent factors that they cannot control or even forecast. The next minicase provides an example.

Minicase 2: "Everyone clapped when I said it"

It was late September 2021 and the two candidates for governor of Virginia were squaring off in a televised debate. Popular former governor Terry McAuliffe was running again, and he was in the lead. During the debate, McAuliffe's opponent brought up a veto that McAuliffe had issued many years prior, of a 2016 bill that would have allowed parents to opt their children out from reading school-assigned sexually explicit books. McAuliffe defended his veto – and then doubled down with the fatal line:

I'm not going to let parents come into schools and take books out … I don't think parents should be telling schools what they should teach.[a]

This statement reverberated nationwide. Immediately, McAuliffe's opponent put out massive negative advertising featuring this statement. McAuliffe started losing ground in the polls.

A few days later, in an effort to control the message, McAuliffe appeared on NBC's "Meet the Press" and defended himself by

---

[6] From *Heart of a Patriot* by Max Cleland, quoted from Muir and Siegel (2009).

noting that "Everyone [i.e., the live audience in the televised debate] clapped when I said it."[b] But that was a feeble defense. The negative ads kept hammering on the issue of parental involvement in the curriculum and, in November, McAuliffe lost the election.

[a] Sept. 29, 2021, www.youtube.com/watch?v=Mcok-vGxYnA&t=1792s

[b] https://nypost.com/2021/11/01/mcauliffe-claims-everybody-clapped-after-classroom-comment/

Let's review what happened. Back in 2016, McAuliffe had vetoed an education bill. At the time, the veto had not received much media attention. Five years later, however, a national debate was raging over the power of school boards over parents. In 2021, schools in the United States were locked down due to the Covid pandemic and parents were furious at the "education establishment." Within this new context, this particular veto became the issue that cost McAuliffe the election.

The Elected Official's Nightmare This kind of situation is every elected official's nightmare. Something they did in the past and seemed unproblematic at the time, can later be redefined by their political opponent as an evil deed. It does not matter that the action may have been uncontroversial back when it was taken. If that redefinition is successful – and it certainly was in McAuliffe's case – the elected official is put in jeopardy and has to choose between two unappealing options: Either disown the earlier action, or defend it. Either way, there is hurt.

This problem is acute for all elected officials because they are continually required to make many decisions comparable, in terms of political risk, to the veto decision that Governor McAuliffe made in 2016. Elected officials face constant pressures to act, both from their constituents and from their own party. Inaction is simply not feasible, but any choice they make, no matter how popular or reasonable in the moment may, with a small probability, become controversial in the future in a way that is difficult to anticipate. If this happens, the issue will likely be seized upon by their challenger in the next election.

Status Quo Bias This kind of radical uncertainty about future scenarios makes elected officials very cautious about taking positions and making decisions. This cautious attitude induces a status quo bias in policy. If they must act, elected officials are disproportionately attracted to those actions that are least likely to be controversial now and in the future. These are the policies that, in the present, are favored by large majorities of constituents.

Elected Officials Need Large Coalitions   From an elected official's perspective, a large coalition's support for a policy is the best presently available evidence that his/her support for that policy will not come back to bite them in the next election. This is why elected officials need large coalitions. From a business perspective, then, the way to influence elected officials is to present them with a large coalition of motivated constituents.

Learning Points   Elected officials are motivated by reelection. When running for reelection, an incumbent faces a challenger who will focus his/her attacks on the incumbent's past mistakes, or simply on what went wrong for whatever reason. This incentive system gives elected officials a strong status quo bias: It makes them fearful of initiating or supporting change. What persuades an elected official to support a new policy is a large coalition of societal interests who favor that policy.

4.3 HOW CORPORATIONS ADVOCATE WITH ELECTED OFFICIALS

The advocacy role of business is viewed with suspicion by the public because, in the public's perception, business advocacy is equated with corruption. This perception is largely inaccurate. I argue here that, contrary to public perception, business influence on elected officials in the United States does not arise through a corrupt exchange of money or favors for policies. Instead, it arises through what I call *business advocacy* (refer to Definition 2 at page 2).

Not Money but Lobbying   The popular view that corporations purchase influence by giving politicians a lot of money or favors is wrong, at least as pertains to the United States. We know this because, if it were true, there would be no need for SBM and all the cases in Chapter 2 would have been much shorter: They would all read "... and the policy went to the highest bidder!"

Jesting aside, there is actually empirical evidence that the business sector spends very little on campaign contributions, both in absolute terms and relative to lobbying expenditures. For example, the pharmaceutical industry, which is arguably the most politically influential industry in Washington, gave less than $12 million per year in federal campaign contributions during the period 1999–2018, against industry revenues of

$345 billion in 2018.[7] This is a negligible amount compared to more than $350 million that the industry spent on lobbying in the year 2021.[8] Going beyond the pharmaceutical industry, Fowler et al. (2020) document that the median publicly traded company contributes very little money to political campaigns: about $4,000 per election cycle.[9] This is a minuscule amount compared to the more than $2.5 billion spent on lobbying by corporations in any given year.[10] In other words, monetary contributions are a small channel of influence for US corporations.

Second, in politics, monetary contributions to political campaigns don't seem to buy corporations that much. Indeed, the academic literature fails to find large returns to political contributions. For example, in a qualitative study of interest mobilization on more than 100 federal issues based on more than 300 interviews with lobbyists and government officials, Baumgartner et al. (2009) summarize a key finding as follows. "We will explore in detail whether the wealthy typically win in Washington, and to the surprise of many readers we will show that they often do not."[11]

More recent quantitative analysis by Fowler et al. (2020) also finds that corporate contributions do not yield meaningful returns for the firms that make them. To reach this conclusion, the authors compare the stock price (cumulative abnormal returns) of firms whose politician (i.e., the politician that they contribute to) goes on to win election, with firms whose politician ends up losing the election. The difference between these two treatments – win vs lose the election – on the firm's stock price is statistically zero, even though the dataset contains a very large number of observations.[12] The conclusion is that contributing to a successful candidate does not affect the firm's value.

In sum, the informed consensus is that corporate campaign contributions are relatively small, and have a negligible return for the corporations

---

[7] Over the entire period, the industry's contributions were $22 million for presidential candidates and $214 million for congressional candidates. Summing, and dividing by twenty years, yields $11.8 million. See Wouters (2020).

[8] Opensecrets.org www.opensecrets.org/federal-lobbying/industries?cycle=2021

[9] These figures do not include Super PAC spending, which is a substitute for campaign contributions. In recent years, these entities have attained high spending levels, about one-third of lobbying expenditures; see Bombardini and Trebbi (2020). However, according to Herrnson and Heerwig (2021, p. 4.) business interests sponsor only 3 percent of Super PACs.

[10] Smith and Keenan (2018).

[11] Baumgartner et al. (2009, p. 20). See, also, Mahoney and Baumgartner (2015) and the literature cited therein.

[12] To be precise, 164,525 firm-candidate-election pairings. See Fowler et al. (2020), p. 848.

making them. For corporations, it is the case that "money can't buy me love."

Lobbying as Coalition Subsidy Lobbying expenditures represent money paid to ex-politicians to advocate with current politicians. What benefit, if any, do current politicians derive from being lobbied? The consensus in political science is that corporations, through their lobbyists, are able to give government officials additional resources to accomplish what the officials wanted to do in the first place. Hall and Deardorff (2006) call this kind of contribution a "legislative subsidy":

In sum, lobbyists freely but selectively provide labor, policy information, and political intelligence to like-minded but resource-constrained legislators. Legislators, in turn, should seek policy-relevant services from like-minded lobbyists. The effect is to expand legislators' effort at making progress toward a policy objective that lobbyists and legislators share.[13]

Along similar lines, in the words of Mahoney and Baumgartner (2105):

individual lobbying organizations cannot "buy friends" in Washington ... the mobilization of government officials simply does not come that cheap. By contrast, we do expect that officials will be sensitive to the overall distribution of material resources mobilized on the issues that are presented to them. They do indeed want to be part of a winning side, and they do indeed like to work on issues where they expect to win.

What Mahoney and Baumgartner (2105) are saying is that government officials cannot be bought off, but they will gladly join a winning coalition if one is presented to them. In sum, corporate lobbyists operate by creating coalitions of Interests, as described in Chapter 5, and by persuading regulators as described in Chapter 7. This is precisely business advocacy as in Definition 2.

A Little Lobbying Goes a Long Way Although lobbying is effective, American corporations do not spend much money on lobbying, either. For example, the pharmaceutical industry's yearly lobbying expenditures, inclusive of lobbying and campaign contributions, while large in absolute value, represented a negligible fraction – less than one thousandth – of industry revenues.[14] More broadly, in the United States as a whole, total lobbying expenditure per year over the years 2010–20 amounted to

---

[13] Hall and Deardorff (2006), p. 75.
[14] Industry revenues exceeded $345 billion in 2018; see Wouters (2020). As mentioned earlier, the industry spent around $350 million on lobbying in the year 2021, which is roughly one-thousandth of 2018 revenues.

roughly $3 billion per year, against a GDP of more than $15 trillion.[15] These facts have led political scientists Stephen Ansolabehere and James M. Snyder of Harvard University, and John M. de Figueiredo of Duke University, to publish an article titled "Why Is There So Little Money in U.S. Politics?"[16]

The reason why corporations don't spend more money on lobbying may be that the returns to pouring money into lobbying diminish rapidly. Perhaps this is because, after an argument has been made to a government official once, not much is gained by repeating the same argument over and over.

Learning Points Most of the business sector's advocacy with elected officials takes place through lobbying, not through campaign donations. Corporate lobbyists operate by helping elected officials create powerful coalitions of interest groups.

4.4 TAKEAWAYS FROM THIS CHAPTER

Elected officials are strictly accountable to their median constituent through elections. Elected officials operate in an environment of radical uncertainty, so they have a strong preference for the status quo. A large coalition of societal interest groups is required to persuade elected officials to support change. Corporate advocacy, in practice, is rarely a corrupt exchange of money for policies. Mostly, it is the provision of information and of other resources that help elected officials create coalitions to enact their favored policies.

---

[15] OpenSecrets (2022).
[16] Ansolabehere et al. (2003).

5

Coalition Building

Politics makes strange bedfellows.

Proverbial saying

A coalition is a collection of like-minded Interests. (Note: Capitalized terms are used in the technical sense of the 4Is.) These are agents – individuals, businesses, non-profits, NGOs, etc. – who are like-minded with respect to an Issue.

Definition 8 (Coalition) *A coalition is a collection of Interests who are like-minded with respect to an Issue.*

This chapter discusses what makes a coalition of interest groups powerful with elected officials, and why a coalition builder is necessary to turn a disparate set of Interests into an influential coalition. The chapter also provides a tool called Coalition Dashboard which, for a given policy agenda, helps to visually assess the power of pro and con coalitions.

5.1 WHAT MAKES A COALITION POWERFUL

What Makes Coalitions Powerful? If a business or an industry wants its policy agenda to be influential with elected officials, it needs to create a powerful coalition that supports the agenda. The coalition may comprise voters and/or of other organizations (unions, firms, nonprofits, etc.) that can mobilize voters in the next election. What makes a coalition powerful? Framework 2 lists the factors that make a coalition powerful with elected officials.

Framework 2: Factors that make a coalition powerful with elected officials

A coalition of Interests forms around an Agenda – the legislative or regulatory change it pursues. The coalition is powerful with elected officials if the following fundamentals hold strongly:

- **Motivation:** The coalition members are highly motivated, meaning that the Agenda is important enough for them to take action now, or to affect how they will act in the next election.
- **Influence:**
  - *Numbers/resources:* The coalition members represent a large fraction of voters, or they can mobilize resources – such as money, activists, or favorable media coverage – that can help the official get many votes in the next election.
  - *Coordinated message:* The Interests in the coalition are united in the pursuit of their policy goal – the Agenda. Every interest group communicates the same short and simple message to elected officials.

Henceforth, I will capitalize a term when it is worth emphasizing that the term is used in the technical sense of Framework 2.

Framework 2 mentions an Agenda, whereas Definition 8 refers to an Issue. What is the difference between Agenda and Issue? They are very similar: In any given setting, they are the change in the rules of the game that is at issue. For now, we can think of them as the same. I will discuss the subtle difference between the two at page 58.

The Motivation of an individual member of an interest group is proportional to the individual agent's gain or loss if the Agenda is implemented, relative to the alternative. Usually, the alternative is the status quo. This gain can be of a material nature, such as earnings for a business or prosperity for citizens, but it can also be of a psychological nature, such as better alignment with moral values. If the gain or loss is large for an agent, that agent will be highly motivated to take action for or against the Agenda. Taking action can mean speaking up on social media, voting on the basis of the Issue in the next election, contributing money to the cause, marching in support of the Agenda, and so on. We care about motivation because, ultimately, we seek to predict whether members of an interest group will take action.

A coalition's Influence results from its members' Numbers/resources, and from the degree of Coordination among its members. Numbers/resources capture many different things. They include votes and, also, activities that ultimately shift votes: community activism, get-out-the-vote efforts, favorable media coverage, campaign contributions, and so on. Numbers/resources matter only insofar as they produce votes in the next election.

If a coalition lacks coordination, it will not be influential. This is because, without coordination, even like-minded Interests will nevertheless have many different individual asks. Faced with many different individual asks, an elected official will not see a way to do something that satisfies all the asks simultaneously. Immediately, the elected official will lose interest.

Checking the Fundamentals in Framework 2 for the Volcker Rule Case

In the Volcker Rule case of Section 2.1, the rule's proponents were able to put together a powerful coalition – more powerful than the financial industry's coalition. The Volcker Rule's proponents had: Huge Numbers of voters on their side who were furious about the crisis; highly Motivated activists – including the "Occupy" movement and, on the opposite side of the political spectrum but on the same side of the Volcker Rule agenda, the Tea Party – that pressured politicians. Coordination was provided by the Obama administration and top levels of the bureaucracy. Conversely, the Volcker Rule's opponents could count on very few voters, and they did not have highly motivated activists on their side. Therefore, Framework 2 suggests that the Volcker Rule's proponents should be able to put together a much more powerful coalition than the financial industry could.

From the coalition building perspective, it is notable that activists *from both ends of the political spectrum*, from "Occupy Wall Street" on the left to the Tea Party on the right, agreed that bailing out the financial industry was outrageous. In the eyes of an elected official, this kind of bipartisan consensus makes for a strong coalition because it makes it less likely that a shift in the narrative could occur in the future that would make the official regret his/her support of the Volcker Rule.[1] Indeed, the narrative did not shift: To this day, the 2008 government bailouts of the financial

---

[1] Refer to the discussion of shifting Overton windows at page 139.

industry are unpopular – despite the fact that the bailouts actually ended up making a lot of money for the government.[2]

Voters Are the MVP The voting public is the Most Valuable Partner (MVP) in any coalition. The Volcker Rule case illustrates the importance of public opinion.

Early on in the financial crisis, the Obama administration had opposed the Volcker Rule because it saw it as unhelpful and difficult to administer.[3] However, as the crisis unfolded, the Obama administration started worrying about being seen as too cozy with the financial industry. At the time, the financial industry as a whole was deeply unpopular because many Americans regarded the industry as culpable for the financial crisis. To prevent being portrayed as pro-finance in the court of public opinion, the Obama administration switched from opposing to supporting the Volcker Rule. A revealing detail illustrates how much public opinion resented the financial industry at the time: During the period when the Volcker Rule was being put together in Congress, lawmakers actually stopped interacting with financial industry lobbyists. This is highly unusual because financial industry lobbyists normally enjoy broad access to lawmakers. In that moment, however, the eyes of public opinion were focused on the lawmakers, and meeting with industry lobbyists would have seemed inappropriate.[4] After the law had been passed, however, and the gaze of public opinion had shifted elsewhere, the industry once again enjoyed broad access to lawmakers and regulators. This observation reveals that the interaction between the rule makers and the financial industry, and therefore the industry's ability to create coalitions, changed dramatically depending on whether public opinion was engaged or not. Clearly, voters were MVP in the coalition of Volcker Rule proponents.

Voters were the MVP in the "World Without Free Knowledge" case of Section 2.6, also. In that case, when media coverage focused the public's attention on the issue of IP rights or, as Google articulated it, web censoring, legislators had no alternative but to comply with public opinion. Indeed, recall that, before the public became aware of the issue, the majority of legislators were actually on the record as supporting

---

[2] ProPublica estimates that \$635 billion was spent on bailing out the US private sector, and, as of August 30, 2021, the government got back \$743 billion, for a gain of about \$109 billion. Figures from https://projects.propublica.org/bailout/, accessed January 23, 2022.

[3] Cassidy (2010).

[4] See Lucchetti and Paletta (2010).

IP protection. However, on the very day when public opinion became engaged with the issue, legislators suddenly reversed their positions.

In sum, as far as elected officials are concerned, voters are the MVP provided that they are engaged. If public opinion is aroused in favor of or against a policy, we should expect elected officials to follow public opinion. However, depending on circumstances and media coverage, the public's attention is fleeting: It rarely centers on an issue for very long. So the influence of public opinion waxes and wanes. For example, in normal times public opinion is not focused on financial regulation, and so public opinion does not shape financial regulation. However, during the financial crisis Americans were focused on financial regulation, and thus public opinion shaped the legislation in that time period. To repeat, voters are the MVP, *provided that their attention is engaged.* Chapter 6 discusses public opinion strategies aimed at engaging the voters' attention.

Learning Points A coalition is powerful with elected officials if its members are numerous, motivated, and they all deliver the same message – meaning, what exactly they want done – to elected officials. The most influential coalition partner with elected officials is the voting public, but the public is not often engaged. I devote a whole chapter to public opinion (Chapter 6).

5.2 BUILDING POWERFUL COALITIONS

For a coalition to be powerful, it must be more than just a loose collection of Interests (in the language of the 4Is) who feel similarly about an Agenda. There must be a coalition builder, whom I will call a policy entrepreneur, who shapes the Agenda and coordinates the coalition. These are the two fundamental elements listed in Framework 2 at page 50 that are actually under the policy entrepreneur's control. I discuss agenda shaping next, then I will discuss coordination. Last, I will discuss who should build the coalition.

Shaping the Agenda A coalition forms around, and in support of, an Agenda. In most cases, the agenda in malleable: It can be shaped. If the agenda is shaped properly, it can catalyze a coalition that is broad and, at the same time, motivated. The Agenda must be shaped to bring on board as many Motivated coalition members as possible, while minimizing the power of the opposing coalition.

Shaping the Agenda in the Recyclers Case In the Recyclers case of Section 2.2, the Agenda had at least two possible versions: a narrow and a broad one. The narrow version of the Agenda was to amend, but not repeal, the Superfund program. The amendment would clarify that scrap is not waste and, therefore, that the recyclers' activity was not covered by the Superfund legislation. This Agenda amounted to a narrow carve-out for the recycling industry: The industry would shed the legal liability and transfer it to other parties, mainly the industrial customers who had bought the recyclers' products. This version of the Agenda was narrow because it let the recyclers off the hook, but it did not go so far as repealing the Superfund program entirely. This narrow scope made it possible for environmental groups to support the Agenda, but it excluded large and powerful industrial interests that, on their part, sought a complete repeal of Superfund. The broad version of the Agenda would have been to repeal the Superfund program entirely. This version of the agenda would have secured powerful coalition partners (big industry) but, also, would have raised intense opposition from environmental groups.

Both agendas were plausible, but they gave rise to very different coalitions, so a choice was necessary. The director of the recyclers' trade association agonized between these two Agenda versions. In the end, he chose the narrow Agenda. This meant opting for environmental groups as coalition partners, and forgoing big industry. This Agenda choice was controversial because, at the time, environmentalists were a "strange bedfellow" for the scrap recycling industry. In hindsight, though, it the director made the right call: The Superfund program was not repealed and, to this day, it is still on the books. But the recycling industry got the carve-out it needed. In sum, ISRI's director opted for a narrow Agenda that jettisoned some powerful coalition partners because the broad Agenda would have catalyzed a strong opposing coalitions.

This case illustrates that Agendas are malleable: They can be shaped. Different versions of an Agenda can bring different partners on board a coalition and, at the same time, affect the composition and strength of the opposing coalition.

Achieving Coordination   The "proof of the pudding" of agenda-shaping is that all coalition members are enthusiastic about giving the same simple message to the rule makers. This is what is referred to as Coordination in Framework 2 at page 50.

Achieving coordination is difficult because, typically, individual coalition members have somewhat different goals, so even the best possible Agenda represents a compromise. Because a compromise Agenda is not anyone's first-best outcome, different coalition members will tend to go off-message and voice different views and requests about what ought to be done. Coordination is not even guaranteed within members of the same interest group: When the interest group is composed of many citizens, for example, coordination is difficult unless mass media are involved. Without coordination, therefore, the danger is sending mixed signals to the Institution. Faced with mixed signals, elected officials will give in to their status quo bias and do nothing.

The degree of coordination that can be achieved is highly situation-specific. It depends, in part, on the Interests' motivation levels, Resources, and on many other factors, too. In general, Coordination is easier when the coalition is composed of a few large firms, especially if the firms operate in the same industry. Coordination is easier, too, when the coalition members are similarly situated and highly motivated. In Framework 8 at page 119, I present a full list of factors that make it easier for an industry coalition (such as the recyclers) to stick together. While that list is presented in a context where the Issue is self-regulation, the same factors also make it easier to Coordinate the Interests for any Issue. I will return to this point at page 123.

Achieving Coordination in the Volcker Rule Case   A good example of the challenges of achieving coordination is provided by the Volcker Rule case of Section 2.1. The financial industry coalition included diverse Interests: hedge funds, which executed the banks' proprietary trading and had the most to lose from the Volcker Rule; large banks, who were the main target of the regulation; and, finally, small community banks who were not the target of the regulation and were more sympathetic than Wall Street behemoths. This diversity of Interests suggests that it would be difficult for the financial industry coalition to speak with a single voice. Indeed, we now know that the financial industry was not able to lobby with a single voice: the hedge funds, represented by the Managed Funds Association, lobbied separately from the American Banking Association, which represented small banks; and large banks lobbied individually.[5] In the end, the community banks benefited from going it alone: They were able to get an exemption from the Volcker Rule.[6] Like in the Recyclers case, the most vulnerable interest group lobbied for a carve-out, and got it.

Achieving Coordination in the Recyclers Case   Coordination is easier when the coalition members are similarly situated and highly motivated.

---

[5] Krawiec (2013), Tables 3 and 5.
[6] Gaetano (2019).

In the Recyclers case of Section 2.2, for example, the individual recycling businesses were similarly situated with respect to the legal risk created by the Superfund law. Moreover, the recyclers were highly motivated because they faced nothing short of bankruptcy. Thus, the recyclers had no alternative: They would either succeed together, or fail separately. These conditions made it easy for ISRI's director to devise a simple message that all the CEOs could enthusiastically repeat. The director boiled the message down to two mantras:

"Scrap is not waste,"

and:

"Amend, don't repeal."

The first quote was designed to pithily explain to elected officials that the Superfund law had a glitch. The second quote was designed to succinctly communicate the recyclers' ask: not a wholesale repeal of the Superfund program, as many other industries were asking but, rather, a small amendment that was actually in the spirit of environmental protection. To ensure that the recyclers' message was delivered uniformly, the director trained the CEOs to memorize the two mantras and repeat them verbatim. The recyclers' CEOs participated in "fly-in blitzes" in which they would fly into Washington, DC on the same day and personally deliver the message to their elected representatives.[7]

The uniformity of the message and the in-person delivery by the CEOs were the reasons for the recyclers' success. Both could happen because the recyclers had common interests and no alternatives, in contrast to the financial industry coalition in the Volcker Rule case.

Who Should Build the Coalition? Typically, the coalition builder tends to be an agent that has a very intense Motivation concerning a given Issue. These agents can be politicians, businesses, trade associations, NGOs, and so on. Definition 3 refers to the person or organization that takes the lead in building the coalition as a policy entrepreneur.

In the Recyclers case, for example, the policy entrepreneur was the director of the recyclers' trade association. In the film censorship case

---

[7] The director trained the CEOs to perform a memorable stunt with legislators: The CEO would pocket a stainless steel spoon from one of the Capitol cafeterias and, after starting the meeting with their representative, s/he would theatrically drop the spoon on the floor and declare, "I just created a Superfund site!" The CEO would then explain to the befuddled interlocutor that, if that spoon contained recycled iron, it would be considered a contaminant under Superfund law. This stunt was successfully performed by many CEOs.

of Section 2.3, a trade association was created with the express purpose of preventing government censorship and rolling back local censorship. In that case, the president of the trade association, Will Hays, was the policy entrepreneur. In the Volcker Rule case, there wasn't a policy entrepreneur that was able to coordinate the financial industry coalition in its opposition to the Volcker Rule. As a result, that coalition was not coordinated. In contrast, the coalition that supported the Volcker Rule was coordinated by the Obama administration. In the Pink Viagra case, the policy entrepreneur was a public relations firm retained by Sprout Pharmaceuticals.

Learning Points Policy entrepreneurs build coalitions by shaping an Agenda. The "proof of the pudding" of Agenda-shaping is that all coalition members are enthusiastic about giving the same simple message to the rule makers. This is what is called Coordination in Framework 2 at page 50.

5.3 COALITION DASHBOARD

This section introduces a visual tool called Coalition Dashboard which, for a given Agenda, helps to visually compare the power of the pro and con coalitions. The Coalition Dashboard is based on Framework 2 at page 50, and it helps assess the probability that a given Agenda is implemented by elected officials.

Framework 3: Coalition Dashboard

The constituent elements of the Coalition Dashboard are:

1. **Agenda:** A given legislative or regulatory change that is at issue. Similar to the Issue in the 4Is from Section 3.6.
2. **Interests:** People or organizations that have a stake in the Agenda. Sometimes called interest groups, they are the same as the Interests in the 4Is from Section 3.6.
3. **Bar Height:** Indicates the Motivation level of an individual Interest. Can be positive or negative. Motivation is defined in Framework 2 at page 50.
4. **Bar Color:** Darker color if the members of an interest group collectively have greater Influence as defined in Framework 2 at page 50, that is, they have greater Numbers/resources and are more Coordinated.

The Coalition Dashboard in Framework 3 is represented visually using a bar graph like the one in Figure 5.1, except possibly with a different number of bars.

Agenda in the Coalition Dashboard The *Agenda* has previously appeared in the "Powerful coalitions" framework at page 50 and it is very similar to, and can coincide with, the Issue in the 4Is framework. The difference, where it exists, is that an Agenda is specific to a coalition and is designed strategically so that all coalition members are able to embrace it and support it (agenda-shaping is discussed at pages 53 and ff.). As such, the Agenda is a sort of "customized Issue," where the customization is necessary to attract, retain, and motivate coalition partners. In fact, the Coalition Dashboard can be used by a policy entrepreneur as a tool to identify a successful Agenda – see page 64.

Interests in the Coalition Dashboard The Interests are exactly the same as in the 4Is, except that the Coalition Dashboard also specifies which Interests are favorable to the Agenda, and which are against.

Bar Height in the Coalition Dashboard The height of a vertical bar represents the Motivation level of an individual agent that is part of an interest group. The motivation level is proportional to the agent's benefit (or loss) if the Agenda is implemented: If the gain or loss is large relative to the status quo, the individual will be highly motivated to take action. I speak intentionally of *individual* agent to emphasize that, as regards Motivation, the unit of analysis is the individual person or organization that is capable of political action. For example, in Figure 5.1, the height of "Citizens with debt" bar represents an *individual citizen's* propensity to act politically (participate in a protest, or vote a certain way in the next election) in support of the Agenda. The focus is on individual motivation because, ultimately, we seek to predict individual actions. Interests whose motivation is very low or who have negligible influence with the Institution may be omitted from the Coalition Dashboard.

Bar Color in the Coalition Dashboard A vertical bar's color value (darker or lighter) represents how Influential, collectively, an interest group is. According to Framework 2 at page 50, this means how many resources an interest group as a whole can command; and how coordinated the individual agents within the interest group are. Note that color value captures a *group property*, that is, a property of the group of agents that comprise an interest group, whereas bar height captures an *individual characteristic* of each agent within that group.

The degree of coordination within an interest group is highly situational. For example, citizens may or may not be coordinated on a given Agenda. The Coalition Dashboard requires one to make educated assumptions about the likelihood that an interest group is coordinated, or that it will be after the coalition is formed.

Coordination across Interests in the Coalition Dashboard   Coordination across, as opposed to within Interests, is an important determinant of a coalition's power. The degree of Coordination both within and across Interests depends, in part, on the skills of the policy entrepreneur – refer to the discussion of coordination at pages 54 and ff. The Coalition Dashboard lacks a graphical way to represent Coordination across Interests. To circumvent this limitation, one can display coalitions of Interests, rather than individual Interests, in the Coalition Dashboard. In Figure 5.1, for example, if hypothetically "Citizens without debt" and "Big banks" had managed to form a coordinated coalition, we could have replaced these two vertical bars with a single bar labeled "Coalition of citizens and banks."

Institution in the Coalition Dashboard   There is no place in the Coalition Dashboard that requires one to specify whether the Institution is elected officials or regulators. This is because the Coalition Dashboard tool is mainly relevant when the Institution is elected officials.[8] Regulators, at a first approximation, do not respond to coalition of voters, so the entire notion of coalition analysis becomes moot when regulators are the Institution.[9]

Interpreting in the Coalition Dashboard   The purpose of the Coalition Dashboard is to help answer the question: Which coalition is more powerful? Or, which is the same, is there a high likelihood that the Agenda is implemented? The answer to these questions is obtained by eyeballing the Coalition dashboard and assessing the depth of color in favor of the Agenda (above the horizontal axis) vs against it (below the horizontal axis). If there is more gray color above the horizontal axis (high gray bars, and deep gray color) than below the horizontal axis, then the Agenda is likely to be implemented. Else, the Agenda is not likely to be implemented and the status quo is likely to persist.

Learning Points   The Coalition Dashboard tool is a useful visual aid to forecast the likelihood that an Agenda will be implemented based on the

[8] By construction, the "Powerful coalitions" box at page 50, which is the basis of the Coalition Dashboard, explicitly mentions elected officials in the box title

[9] However, this is not a hard-and-fast rule: Occasionally, it can be helpful to use the Coalition Dashboard to keep track of the Influence of different Interests on regulators, as I do at page 65.

relative strength of the opposing coalitions. The Coalition Dashboard is based on Framework 2 at page 50.

5.4 HOW TO BUILD THE COALITION DASHBOARD

Let's practice building the Coalition Dashboard for the Agenda of student debt relief in Section 2.4. We want to assess whether, at the time when the big banks were contemplating an exit from the student loan market, they were facing a threateningly powerful opposing coalition in favor of debt relief. Clearly, such an assessment would be a significant factor in the big banks' decision to exit the market. The finished product is displayed in Figure 5.1.

Agenda in the Student Debt Relief Case　The first step in building a Coalition Dashboard is to explicitly state the Agenda, which is the specific policy change that is at issue. The Agenda is displayed in the top-left corner of the Coalition Dashboard. In our case, the Agenda is debt relief. Debt relief, however, is not a sufficiently specific Agenda to guide strategy. We need to know whether the relief was expected to come from elected officials or from regulators because, in the latter case, the Coalition Dashboard may not be the right tool.[10] In our case, debt relief involved such a broad cross section of the population, was so economically significant, and so morally charged, that any changes will have to be decided by elected officials even if, formally, the relief came in the form of a regulatory change. Therefore, the Agenda must be stated as: debt relief by elected officials. Then, we know that the Coalition Dashboard is an appropriate tool in this case. We must also specify whether the relief is expected to come at the expense of the government or of the big banks. In what follows I assume the latter.

Societal Interests in the Student Debt Relief Case　Societal Interests are listed at the bottom of the graph in Figure 5.1. These are the agents that have a stake in the Agenda. In the student loan case, there were at least three types of Interests: citizens who had student debt, citizens who did not have student debt, and the banks that were holding the debt. (At the time of our case the debt was still held by banks.) Note that legislators are not listed because we do not, as a general rule, list Institutions among the Interests: This rule is inherited from the 4Is in Section 3.6.

Bar Height Represents the Motivation Level　Once the Agenda has been specified, we are in a position to assess which societal Interests favor the

---

[10] Recall that, as a first approximation, the Coalition Dashboard is only relevant when elected officials are the Institution, see page 59.

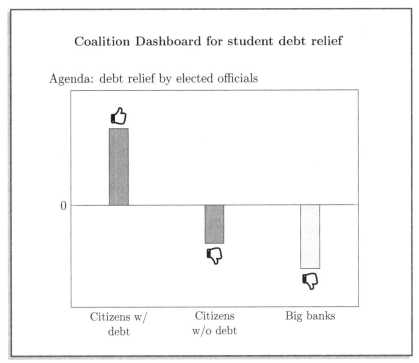

FIGURE 5.1 Coalition Dashboard for the student debt relief case in Section 2.4. Bar height above (resp., below) zero represents the motivation level in favor of (resp., against) the Agenda. Thumbs-up (resp., down) indicate support for the Agenda (resp., the status quo). Darker gray color represents greater influence.

Agenda, which oppose it, and how intensely they feel about it. Each Interest's Motivation level is depicted by the height of its bar in Figure 5.1. So, for example, citizens with debt are depicted as having the highest motivation level (tallest bar) among all Interests, whereas citizens without debt have the lowest motivation level (shortest bar). The height of the bar records the *individual citizen's* Motivation level. Note, too, that the bars of citizens without debt lies *below* the zero line, indicating that each of these citizens has *negative* motivation for the agenda; that is, they *oppose* it. Banks are depicted as having the most negative Motivation, that is, being the most opposed to the Agenda. For added emphasis, I used a thumbs-up symbol to denote support, and a thumbs-down to denote opposition to the Agenda.

Determining Bar Height The height of each bar in Figure 5.1 reflects a holistic evaluation of the willingness of members of an interest group to take action in the beyond-market arena. Admittedly, there is no numerical formula to derive the precise height of the bars. A given bar height is best understood in relation to the height of the other Interests' bars.

How is the height of each bar determined? For a citizen with debt, I reasoned that s/he would be very highly motivated to obtain debt relief: Recall that the median debtor owed more than $20,000. Sums of this magnitude are very significant – sometimes, even existential – for the average American. So, I gave these citizens the tallest bar. For banks, I reckoned that a bank's motivation would be highly negative but, in absolute size (i.e., in terms of the distance in either direction from the zero line) not as large as for a citizen who is in debt. This is because student debt relief, while painful, was not an existential issue for most big banks: After all, when debt relief became likely the banks had the option to sell the debt to other institutions, albeit at a loss. So I gave members of this interest group a negative bar of medium size.

For citizens without debt, I reasoned that they would be opposed to debt relief for two reasons. First because, as taxpayers, they would bear the financial cost of debt relief. Second, because any citizen who had incurred student debt and paid it off might feel duped. On the other hand, some of them would be friendly with some debt relief beneficiaries. Overall, after taking these conflicting considerations into account, I judged that these citizens would be mildly or somewhat opposed to debt relief, but not majorly so. Hence, I assigned them a negative bar of small size.

As I mentioned earlier, there is no numerical formula to derive the precise height of the bars. This is why the framework intentionally omits a numerical scale on the vertical axis. Figure 5.1 should be interpreted as signifying that citizens with debt are much more Motivated to act in the beyond-market arena than citizens without debt. In practice, this means that the former are probably willing to attend a march in favor of debt relief, and will vote for any presidential candidate that promises debt relief, whereas the latter may not respond to this issue as much. As for banks, their bar height indicates that a bank will invest some resources and lobbying time in opposing student debt relief, but not to the exclusion of all other issues.

Determining Bar Color   Not all bars in Figure 5.1 have the same color value: Some are darker (dark gray, for citizens); others are lighter (light gray, for big banks). The color's value, that is, its darkness or lightness, represents an interest group's collective Influence, that is, Numbers/

resources and Coordination level. Why did I color the citizens' bar a darker shade than the big banks' bar? At page 52, I wrote that voters are the MVP whenever they are engaged. Are voters likely to be engaged on the issue of student debt relief? Yes. For one thing, the density of people touched by the debt issue is high in American society: 30 percent of the population, or more if we count spouses, parents, and so on – refer back to Section 2.4. Many of these people have high Motivation, so any prospects of student debt relief is likely to be discussed with family and among friends. Second, the issue of debt forgiveness has a deep moral valence that makes it highly viral in public discourse. These two factors make it likely that the media will report extensively, activist groups will get involved, and politicians will take position. So we can expect public opinion to be engaged. This is why citizens are given a very dark color value.

In comparison to engaged citizens, banks have relatively little Influence. Yes, banks have numbers (many employees) and resources (lots of money and expertise). And yes, banks are highly Coordinated: They have their trade associations and, moreover, the big banks are few, so it is not difficult for their CEOs to coordinate.[11] But, even taking all this into consideration, when public opinion is engaged, banks are comparatively irrelevant: See the discussion at page 52 in the context of the Volcker Rule. This is why the banks' bar is colored light gray as opposed to dark gray.

Overall Assessment of Relative Power in the Student Debt Relief Case
Visual examination of Figure 5.1 indicates the following. A large fraction of Americans have a strong financial interest in actively supporting debt relief. The rest have a weaker financial interest against debt relief. Many of the latter will be persuaded, in either direction, by the moral valence of the issue in public discourse (see Chapter 6 for a discussion of morality in public discourse). The financial industry is expected to be relatively uninfluential in the ultimate outcome. Overall, the debt relief agenda has a strong chance of being persuasive with elected officials. This analysis suggests that the big banks made a good call in exiting the student loan market.

Learning Points   The Coalition Dashboard is a useful tool to assess the relative strengths of opposing coalitions. The Coalition Dashboard for

---

[11] With this being said, bank advocacy is surprisingly decentralized in the United States: See the discussion at page 55.

the student debt case (Figure 5.1) indicates that the debt relief agenda has a strong chance of being persuasive with elected officials. Therefore the big banks made a good call in exiting the student loan market.

5.5 COMPARING DIFFERENT COALITION DASHBOARDS

While Figure 5.1 represents a single Coalition Dashboard, the Coalition Dashboard framework can also be used in a compare-and-contrast analysis. This is done by building different Coalition Dashboards for: different Agendas, different economic environments, or different Institutions.

In general, when comparing two Coalition Dashboards that differ in the Institution but share the same Agenda and economic setting, bar heights will be the same across the two Dashboards because the Interests' Motivation levels are the same, but bar colors will likely differ because each Interest's Influence depends on the Institution. Conversely, when comparing two Coalition Dashboards that share the same Institution, bar colors will be the same across the two Dashboards, but bar heights will likely differ.

Examples and benefits of comparing different Coalition Dashboards are discussed next.

Different Agendas Comparing Coalition Dashboards across different Agendas can help a policy entrepreneur pick the best agenda. In the Recyclers case, for example, the environmental groups were favorable to the narrow agenda ("amend, don't repeal") but unfavorable to the broad one (repeal Superfund entirely) – see page 53. Building the Coalition Dashboards generated by each agenda and comparing them indicates that the narrow Agenda created a potentially more powerful coalition than the broad Agenda.

Different Economic Environments Comparing Coalition Dashboards across different economic environments is done in Figure 12.1 at page 167. The comparison reveals that a given Agenda (price regulation) is more popular in scenario (a) than in scenario (b).

Different Institutions Comparing Coalition Dashboards across different Institutions can help a policy entrepreneur select a favorable Institution. For example, when seeking a license to operate in a city, the CEO of Uber regularly chose to fight in the court of public opinion, where the relevant Institution was the mayor, rather than in the regulatory arena where the Institution was the taxi regulator. Comparing Coalition Dashboards reveals why. Rideshare customers were just one of the taxi regulator's key stakeholders and, in the regulator's mind, their convenience was probably less salient than the taxi industry's concerns over profits. In contrast, rideshare customers were top of mind for the mayor because a large fraction of them were voters. Hence, rideshare customers were probably more influential when the mayor was the Institution, rather than the taxi regulator. Comparing the Dashboards for the two different Institutions reveals that Uber had a better chance of success in the court of public opinion than in the regulatory arena.

A caveat: Comparing across Institutions can be dicey if regulators are one of the Institutions. Indeed, as mentioned at page 59, the Coalition Dashboard framework may be moot when regulators are the Institution. However, this is not a hard-and-fast rule: Occasionally, it can be helpful to use the Coalition Dashboard to keep track of the Influence of different Interests on regulators, as I did above.

Learning Points The Coalition Dashboard framework can be used to compare coalitions across: different Agendas, different economic environments, or different Institutions.

5.6 TAKEAWAYS FROM THIS CHAPTER

A coalition is powerful with elected officials if its members are Motivated and Influential: Refer to the "Powerful coalitions" framework at page 50. Voters, when they are engaged, are the most Influential coalition partner (MVP) with elected officials.

A business or industry that, like the recyclers, needs to influence the rules of the competitive game, must shape an Agenda that maximizes its own coalition's power and minimizes the opposing coalition's power.

For any given Agenda, the Coalition Dashboard is a useful visual aid to assess the relative strengths of opposing coalitions. A businesses that seeks to forecast the evolution of public policy in order to guide its competitive strategy can use the Coalition Dashboard.

6

Public Opinion Strategies

As mentioned in Section 5.1, voters are the MVP of any coalition if they are engaged with the coalitions' Agenda. How should a business publicly articulate its agenda in order to maximize voter engagement? Or, alternatively, how can messaging reduce the public's engagement with the opposing coalition's agenda? This chapter deals with these questions.

In some cases, a business *wants* its voice to be heard in the public arena. This is the case for example, in the "World Without Free Knowledge" case of Section 2.6, when Google and Wiki did want to be heard. This chapter is helpful in these cases and, also, in instances when a business or a coalition does not benefit from communicating its policy agenda to the public. In these instances, the content of this chapter can help anticipate the opposing coalition's public opinion strategy, and even to reduce its effectiveness.

6.1 MORALITY IS THE GRAMMAR OF POLICY

By definition, a business that operates in the beyond-market arena pursues an Agenda; that is, it advocates for or against a specific policy – a tax, a subsidy, a compliance rule, and so on. While the business usually thinks of these agendas in terms of monetary costs and benefits, the public perceives them as part of a moral landscape. In general we, as citizens, perceive policy agendas as morally relevant because they define the kind of society we live in.

For example, consider the following Agenda: Discourage the production of fossil fuels, even if that leads to an increase in transportation costs. How do most people *intuitively* perceive this policy agenda? Those of us who regard the environment as sacred will support it instinctively. Those among us who care more about economic freedom and, perhaps, about the plight of the poor who are most impacted by fuel prices, might instinctively oppose it. The first group of people might then reply that the poor can be made whole by subsidizing public transportation. But this additional policy item may be instinctively abhorrent to those among us who view government expansion as oppressive.

What I am trying to convey is that most people conceptualize policy agendas, such as fossil fuel regulation, in relation to deeply help moral values, including sanctity of the environment and freedom from government oppression. Most people perceive policy through a moral lens. This is not to say that citizens ignore the material implications of policy. In fact, when a policy's material implications are large, citizens tend to "vote with their pocketbook." Even then, however, their attitudes toward policy are conceptualized in moral terms. In other words, in the minds of most people, the spheres of policy and public morality overlap.

This is a good place to clarify that, when using the terms "moral" and "morality," I am not referring to something that is necessarily good, or desirable, or correct. Rather, I am using the term "morality" in a technical sense that means, roughly, "widely shared values": Refer to Definition 9 at page 68.

That people should conceptualize public policy through a moral lens is not surprising. A public policy is, after all, in its simplest essence a set of rules that is coercively enforced by the state. This use of coercion, in the mind of most people, is only justified if the final outcome feels morally right.

What follows from this is that when a business publicly advocates for an Agenda, it is perceived by the public as operating in the moral sphere. Therefore, for the agenda to connect with the public, it must be articulated in the language of morality. The tendency of business, of course, is the opposite: to adopt the language of policy and to shy away from moral language. While this may be a good strategy for communicating with domain experts and legislators, this is not a winning strategy when communicating with the public. Public opinion strategies must appeal to people's moral intuitions, or at least conform with them.

Of course, appealing to moral intuitions is a necessary, not sufficient condition for success. When a policy clearly and significantly harms a group of citizens, they will be unlikely to support it regardless of the language that it is couched in. Still, many policies only impact citizens negligibly, or in ways that are difficult to predict. In these cases, a public opinion strategy can be effective, and then it is important for business to realize that communication, even if spoken in the language of policy, is heard in the language of morality.

Learning Points When a business advocates for an Agenda, it operates in the public sphere which, in the public perception, overlaps with the moral sphere. Therefore, people evaluate policy agendas through a moral lens. Public opinion strategies must connect explicitly with people's moral intuitions.

6.2 BUILDING A MORAL NARRATIVE

A moral narrative, in this book's context, is one that connects an Agenda directly with morality. But what is morality?

What Is a Moral Narrative Here is a definition according to Moral Foundations Theory (MFT).[1]

Definition 9 (Morality, According to Moral Foundations Theory)
Morality is the set of normative standards about behavior whose violation is intuitively understood and emotionally disapproved of by many in a community.

MFT was developed by Jonathan Haidt, a professor of social psychology then at the University of Virginia. Haidt's research agenda was to find out how moral intuitions differ across cultures and people. This was a breathtakingly ambitious research agenda: Haidt was after the very building blocks of human morality. Operationally, Haidt asked thousands of people to fill out a thirty-item "Moral Foundations Questionnaire" (MFQ) featuring questions such as: "When you decide whether something is right or wrong, to what extent do you consider whether or not someone suffered emotionally?" Or: "To what extent do you agree/disagree with the following statement: 'People should be loyal to their family members, even when they have done something wrong'."[2]

Then, Haidt processed the thousands of responses to the questionnaire using a statistical technique called factor analysis. This technique is used to put many questions (in this case, thirty questions) into a few "buckets." Questions that belong to the same bucket share the property that the typical subject's answer to any question in the bucket predicts the

---

[1] Adapted from the first two criteria for foundationhood in Graham et al. (2013, p. 107). See also Haidt (2012).

[2] The MFQ is available at https://moralfoundations.org/questionnaires/.

answers to all other questions in that same bucket. Intuitively, a bucket summarizes all the information elicited by the individual questions in the bucket. The result was six buckets or, in technical language, factors. Knowing where a subject stands on each of these factors provides a full picture of the subject's stance on all thirty questions. Thus MFT was born. The six factors are reproduced in the next box (with their associated emotions).[3]

Framework 4: Moral Foundations (associated emotions)

1. **Care/harm** (compassion for the victim, anger at the perpetrator)
2. **Fairness/cheating** (anger, gratitude, guilt)
3. **Loyalty/betrayal** (group pride, rage at traitors)
4. **Authority/subversion** (respect, fear)
5. **Sanctity/degradation** (disgust)
6. **Liberty/oppression**

Technically, the six factors listed in Framework 4 are just statistical summaries of peoples' responses to a 30-item questionnaire. But, according to MFT, they are much more: They represent a full and concise list of all the moral/sacred values whose violation is intuitively understood and emotionally disapproved of by many in a community. The six factors are intended to capture "the concerns, perceptions, and emotional reactions that consistently turn up in moral codes around the world."[4] According to MFT, these six foundations are, in fact, the building blocks of human morality.[5]

Psychometric studies have established three empirical regularities. First, people differ in how they load on the six foundations. When looking at the same scenario – say, a harsh punishment for violating a norm – some people will primarily focus on the harm done to the person being punished (Foundation 1) and, therefore, find the punishment to be morally objectionable. Others, instead, will focus on norm subversion (Foundation 4) and, therefore, feel that the punishment was called for.

---

[3] Graham et al. (2013, Table 2.1).

[4] Graham et al. (2013, p. 60).

[5] Graham et al. (2013) speculate that these foundations may have an evolutionary basis. For example, the Harm/care foundation might have evolved to promote punishment of those who, within a small group, would not care for other people's children. The Fairness/cheating foundation might have evolved to promote punishment of those who cheat within a bilateral relationship, such as a Prisoner's Dilemma.

This is not surprising: We know from experience that what is morally objectionable to some barely registers with others. This heterogeneity is called "moral pluralism." Second, interestingly, how people load on the six foundations correlates with their political leanings. People who identify as secular liberals load highest on the first two foundations: Care, and Fairness; and relatively low on the other three. Conversely, people who identify as social conservatives load more equally on all six foundations.[6] Third, how a person loads on the six Moral Foundations is highly persistent through time: Research shows that, except for relatively young people, a person's MFQ scores are highly stable over time, even when elicited repeatedly across the span of years.[7] This is reassuring from a scientific perspective because we think of a person's moral values as stable and persistent.

Before we move on, a few comments on these foundations. The Fairness foundation is understood differently by different people: either as equality of outcomes, or as equality of opportunity. Therefore, for some people outcome disparities along racial or gender lines violate Fairness; for other people, race-conscious policies like affirmative action, which aim to reduce outcome disparities, violate Fairness. Also, the Sanctity foundation is not limited to the religious sphere: respect for nature and the environment, for example, are a manifestation of the Sanctity foundation. Furthermore, the sixth foundation, Liberty/oppression, has so far been less well-identified statistically than the other five. Finally, MFT takes no stand on the degree to which an individual's specific loading on the six foundations is innate or, rather, it is environmentally determined.

Translating an Agenda into Moral Language	MFT suggests a procedure to translate an Agenda into moral language. The procedure is: First, identify one or more item in Framework 4 that the agenda connects with; then, translate the benefits and aspirations of the agenda or, alternatively, its risks and downsides, into the language of MFT. Next, I offer some examples of what this translation looks like in practice.

Moral Narrative in NRA Advertisements	The National Rifle Association's (NRA) public opinion campaign is a notable example of a policy agenda that is expressed in moral language (moral, that is, in the sense of Definition 9). For the purpose of this book I stipulate that, broadly speaking, the NRA's Agenda is to oppose firearm regulations. It is not my intention here either to endorse or to criticize this, or any other Agenda.

[6] Graham et al. (2013, p. 84).
[7] Hatemi et al. (2019), Figure 2 and footnote 5.

Rather, I acknowledge that the NRA is a controversial organization. I use its strategy as a pedagogically useful illustration of what it means to translate an Agenda into moral language.

Many, including both supporters and opponents of the NRA's Agenda, view the NRA's public opinion campaign as effective. According to William Vizzard, an academic and former regulator of the firearm industry: "The NRA and its allies have exercised as much control over public policy by molding public attitudes, language, and cultural paradigms as by direct influence in Congress."[8]

To illustrate how the NRA's public opinion campaign translates its Agenda into moral language, it is helpful to track the evolution of the tone and narrative of NRA advertisements over time. Early on, the advertisements did not use a moral language. Later on, they did. This evolution can be detected in the titles of selected NRA advertisements.

Minicase 3: NRA advertisement titles over the years

The following is a list of NRA advertisements titles over the years.[a]

1920: "Rifle shooting is a mighty fine sport. Do you belong to a rifle club?"

1951: "A 50-Cent Junior Membership in the National Rifle Association."

1957: "More fun with your guns!"

1970: "Hunters Beware!"

1973: "Only you can save hunting. . . "

Late 1980s: "Why Can't a Policeman Be There When You Need Him?" and "This is the Most Dangerous Place in America."

1993: "What's the First Step to a Police State?"

2013: "NRA Stand and Fight: Protection for Obama's Children, Gun-Free Zone for Ours?"

2016: "Freedom's Safest Place: You Haven't Met America."

2017: "It's time America Honored Its Police Again," and "We Stand for Freedom."

[a] Sources: Gilson (2013), Beer (2017)

---

[8] Vizzard (1995). William J. Vizzard was an employee of the Bureau of Alcohol, Tobacco and Firearms, which is the regulator of the firearm industry.

Up to 1970, the advertisement titles might be described as happy and light. They did not feature a moral narrative. The 1957 "More fun with your guns!" advertisement read, in part:

... MORE FUN *with* YOUR GUNS!
Over a quarter-million sportsmen invite you to
JOIN – THE NATIONAL RIFLE ASSOCIATION for only $5.00
Yours: A Year's Subscription to the AMERICAN RIFLEMAN Magazine
Yours: MEMBERSHIP IN THE NRA
Yours: A GOLD-FILLED MEMBERSHIP BUTTON

Starting in 1970, the advertisement titles turned dark and ominous. The 1970 "Hunters Beware!" ad read, in part:

Hunters Beware!
If ever there was a time when you needed NRA to help protect your present and future hunting rights ...
That Time Is NOW!
Between you and that threat stands NRA
NRA has to win it – one new member every minute!

The shift in tone is unmistakable. Emotionally, the "Hunters Beware" title feels ominous. In the body of the advertisement, the NRA warned: "There are powerful forces working eagerly ... to abolish the hunting rights you enjoy today" and stated: "Between you and that threat stands NRA."

After 1970, all the advertisement titles connected explicitly with a moral foundation: either the Liberty/Oppression foundation, as did the "Hunters Beware" advertisement, or the Care/harm foundation – by emphasizing that guns afforded vulnerable people protection from criminals.[9] A second, more subtle shift is also worth noting. The language shifted from the personal sphere (individual benefits of membership) to

---

[9] Similarly, a TV advertisement by gun manufacturer Daniel Defense featured a dad driving to his suburban home and finding his wife and infant daughter safe and secure. The voice-over narration said: "My family's safety is my highest priority. I am responsible for their protection, and no-one has the right to tell me how to defend them."

the social sphere (a well-armed citizenry benefits the common good). This shift from the personal to the social sphere was necessary to engage with the sphere of morality – again, I use the term in the technical sense of Definition 9. The narrative became one of mobilizing to fight for something bigger than oneself, maybe defending a way of life for the benefit of all. The tone was that of a call to arms.

The NRA's ability to express its Agenda in moral terms was critical to mobilizing the support of a sizable segment of public opinion. At the same time, another sizable segment of public opinion was turned off by the NRA's language. The result was increased polarization in public discourse. I will return to the issue of polarization later in this chapter.

Moral Narrative in the "World without Free Knowledge" Case   Another example of an Agenda being expressed in moral language is the "World Without Free Knowledge" landing page, which was shown by Wikipedia to protest the SOPA and PIPA bills. That screen read, in part (refer to Figure 2.1): "Right now, the U.S. Congress is considering legislation that could fatally damage the free and open Internet."

Again, a policy agenda is connected to a moral violation (in this case, of the Liberty foundation). Again, the online viewer is issued a "call to arms" and given the opportunity to fight for the common good (freedom) by supporting Wikipedia's Agenda.

Moral Narrative in the Pink Viagra Case   A third example of an Agenda connecting with the sphere of morality is the Pink Viagra case of Section 2.7. To mobilize support for the new drug's approval, Sprout Pharmaceutical focused on gender disparities and unfairness rather than extolling the new drug's virtues. The effect was to articulate a moral violation, in this case, that of the Fairness/cheating foundation (refer to the Moral Foundations framework at page 69), which approving the drug would begin to redress.

Learning Points   A strategy aimed at mobilizing public opinion must express its Agenda in the language of morality. The six Moral Foundations listed in the framework at page 69 are the building blocks of moral narratives. Therefore, a good public opinion strategy must, if it seeks to elicit action, build on at least one of the six Moral Foundations.

The advertisement never directly mentioned or showed a gun, but it did connect powerfully with the Harm and Liberty foundations. The advertisement was produced for display in the 2013 Superbowl, but it was rejected by the National Football League. See www.youtube.com/watch?v=KQLQxnOZmvc&t=62s and Malkin (2013).

6.3 NEGATIVITY IN THE MORAL NARRATIVE

So far, we have seen three examples in which an Agenda was translated into a moral narrative: the NRA's advertisements, Wikipedia's SOPA/PIPA protest, and the Pink Viagra public opinion campaign. In all three cases, the narrative was negative rather than positive, dark rather than light. In all cases, the narrative focused on the threat of a moral violation: of the Liberty foundation in the cases of the NRA and Wikipedia, and of the Fairness foundation in the Pink Viagra case. The language was that of fear and outrage.

Why couldn't these moral narratives accentuate the positive, rather than the negative? The answer cannot simply be that fear-mongering helps maintain the status quo, because the policy goal in the Pink Viagra case was in fact to change the status quo. Instead, the answer lies in a different place: Moral judgment, unfortunately, goes hand in hand with negativity.

Association between Morality and Punishment Social scientists have long noticed an association between morality and punishment. A large literature argues that humans have evolved a taste for so-called "moralistic punishment," that is, the punishment of norm violators even if the punisher has not been harmed.[10] There is evidence of moralistic punishment in the practices of gossip (a mild group punishment for small violations) and shunning (a more serious form of group punishment). Today, social media are often used to "cancel" people and businesses for perceived moral violations – but, significantly, rarely to reward them for moral virtue.[11] Moralistic punishment has even been observed in chimpanzees.[12]

Why the moral sphere should be more closely associated with punishment than with reward is an interesting, though somewhat theoretical question.[13] I speculate that this is because punishment is a cheaper way to provide incentives than rewarding, especially if a moral code is well

---

[10] See Kurzban et al. (2007) for a review.
[11] With the possible exception of the moral virtue of canceling others, which is the exception that proves the rule.
[12] de Waal (1996).
[13] The question is this: If morality is an evolutionary response to the problem of regulating bilateral and small-group relationships, so that the functional purpose of morality is to provide incentives for cooperation and against norm violations, why should the incentives come in the negative form (punishment) rather than in the positive form (reward)?

established so that punishment rarely needs to be meted out.[14] In addition, it may be cheaper and easier to destroy resources than to create them. Regardless, I take it as a given that morality is more closely associated with punishment than with reward.

What matters for our purpose is that humans perceive the moral domain as naturally associated with, and possibly triggering, the act of punishing. If this is the case, then it is natural for a moral narrative to arouse a stronger impulse to punish a moral violator than to reward a righteous person. Put differently, a moral narrative can easily move people to punish, but not so easily to reward.[15]

Why the Moral Narrative in a Public Opinion Strategy Tends toward the Negative With this in mind, it is clear why the NRA, Wikipedia, and Sprout Pharmaceutical all adopted a narratives of fear, outrage, and moral violations. This is because these organizations needed the public to take action, and action is motivated by moral violations, not by moral virtue.

Learning Points Moral virtue does not arouse action; moral violations do. Thus, any public opinion strategy directed at eliciting action from the public must be couched in terms of moral violations. An unsettling implication of this fact is that public discourse on policy issues will, in the majority of cases, be predominantly negative.

6.4 THE DAMPENING EFFECT OF STATISTICS

A moral narrative moves people to act by stirring *emotions* (refer to the Moral Foundations box at page 69). This is intuitive: If people are emotionally aroused they are more likely to, say, take a personally costly action to support a policy agenda. This section shows that, conversely, using the language of policy, that is, presenting data and metrics, actually makes people *less likely* to act in support of a policy agenda. This is remarkable because it suggests that the language of policy is not merely neutral: It actually decreases engagement.

Evidence for this claim comes from a clever laboratory experiment. In the experiment, each participant received five one-dollar bills and a letter asking the participant to donate some of the money to a charity called

---

[14] In the parlance of game theory, providing incentives using rewards is expensive because rewards are "on the equilibrium path," whereas punishment is cheap because it is "out of equilibrium."

[15] Hence, perhaps, the proverbial saying: "Virtue is its own reward."

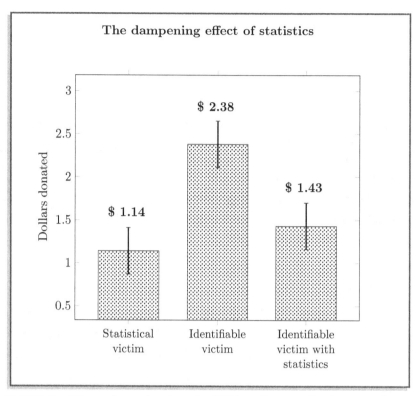

FIGURE 6.1 Money donated to *Save the Children* charity under three experimental treatments. Reproduced from Small et al. (2007).

Save the Children. The content of the letter represented the treatment. In the first treatment, called "statistical victim condition," the letter provided statistical information about the problem of starvation in Africa. In the second treatment, called "identifiable victim condition," the letter showed a picture of a little girl and provided a brief description about her.[16]

The experimental findings are presented in Figure 6.1. Not surprisingly, the "identifiable victim" treatment caused participants to donate significantly more than the "statistical victim" condition ($2.38 vs $1.14, out of a budget of $5). This is what one would expect. In the language of this section, I interpret this finding as evidence that the emotions associated with the harm/care foundation (refer to Framework 4 at page 69) were aroused more intensely when the victim was identifiable (the little girl) than when many victims were described abstractly in the language of

---

[16] Small et al. (2007).

policy. In other words, this finding supports the claim made at the beginning of this section that the language of public policy does not resonate with people.

The most interesting experimental finding is a third treatment, called "identifiable victim with statistics." This treatment combines the first two: In this treatment, the letter showed both the little girl's picture and description, *and* the statistical information about starvation in Africa. Figure 6.1 shows that, in this treatment, participants only gave $1.43, much less than in the identifiable victim treatment and barely more than in the statistical victim treatment. This finding demonstrates that people become deactivated when an argument is presented to them using data, *even in conjunction* with emotionally arousing information. In other words, the language of policy has the power to actually dampen the effect of another narrative that is being put forth in moral language at the same time.[17]

Learning Points   The language of policy, that is, data and metrics, makes people *less likely* to act in support of a policy agenda. Therefore, if the goal of a public opinion strategy is to "fly under the radar" or to tone down the moral valence of existing discourse, presenting data and speaking the language of public policy is the way to go.

6.5 MORAL PLURALISM

As mentioned earlier, psychometric studies have established that people differ systematically in how they load on the moral foundations listed in Framework 4 at page 69. This heterogeneity is called "moral pluralism." Moral pluralism has some unsettling implications for public opinion strategies.

Implications for Public Opinion Strategies   Moral pluralism implies that not everybody responds similarly to a given moral narrative. For example, people who load mostly on the Care and Fairness foundations may not be especially sensitive to violations of the Freedom foundation, such as those highlighted in the NRA advertisements. The fact that people differ systematically in what they consider morally (un)acceptable has an important consequence. Because a policy agenda is understood in moral terms, different people will react differently, perhaps even in diametrically

---

[17] Perhaps, this finding supports the often repeated and chilling quotation, attributed to Joseph Stalin: "the death of one person is a tragedy; the death of one million is a statistic."

opposed ways, to a given public opinion strategy. Therefore, moral pluralism implies that public opinion strategies should not be expected to activate everyone equally. Rather, a public opinion strategy should be expected to activate only those people whose moral foundations are violated.

Learning Points   Because people differ in their moral makeup, a public opinion strategy should not necessarily be expected to resonate with everyone. A public opinion strategy may well mobilize only those people whose moral foundations are violated. Therefore, a moral narrative in the service of a public opinion strategy may well end up being somewhat divisive or polarizing.

6.6 SOCIETAL TRUST AS A PRECONDITION

This section shows that societal trust is important for a public opinion strategy to succeed. This point is illustrated using the "World Without Free Knowledge" case of Section 2.6. Then, a qualifier is added: While important, societal trust is not necessarily essential. This is shown this using the cases of Pink Viagra and the NRA.

Importance of Societal Trust   In Section 2.6, I argued that the proponents of SOPA and PIPA, collectively, were a more powerful coalition than the opponents, at least back when the case took place in 2012. Let me strengthen the argument here. First, the proponents of SOPA and PIPA, that is, American industry, employed more people than the opponents. Second, they had an established and powerful lobbying apparatus, which Google and Wikipedia lacked back then. Third, on its merits, American industry's case *for* SOPA and PIPA was not necessarily any harder to make with the public than Google and Wikipedia's case *against it*. The overwhelming majority of the public knew little or nothing about the content of the bill, whose provisions were, moreover, highly technical. My point is that either narrative, pro- or con- SOPA/PIPA, could have been persuasive with the US public, provided that it connected with one or more of the moral foundations in Framework 4. The narrative pro-SOPA/PIPA could have connected with the care/harm foundation, highlighting the fact that SOPA/PIPA protected vulnerable IP creators (think of an aging country musician relying on royalties for his/her subsistence). The narrative against SOPA/PIPA could connect with the liberty/oppression foundation (threatening free knowledge). Fourth, proponents and opponents were roughly evenly matched in their ability to communicate with voters: Though Google and Wiki controlled America's computer screens, the supporters of SOPA and PIPA controlled traditional media (indeed, they *were* the traditional media).

Overall, therefore, the American industry coalition supporting SOPA and PIPA was at least as powerful as the opposing coalition, or maybe even more so. So why did it lose so decisively? I believe that American industry lost because the public trusted Google and Wikipedia more.

At that time of our case, a survey reveals that technology companies were more trusted than the opposing coalition. To see this, refer to Figure 6.2 which displays trust levels by industry in 2012, the year when the battle over SOPA and PIPA took place. The horizontal bars show the population's response to the question "How much do you trust businesses in this industry to do what's right?" Longer bars indicate greater trust. Industries that supported SOPA and PIPA are marked by a thumbs-up symbol, those that opposed it by a thumbs-down. The figure shows that the tech industry, at the time, was highly trusted. Not so the media and pharmaceutical industries. Therefore, the highly trusted opponents of SOPA and PIPA were able to credibly shape the message to the American public, in a way that the less-trusted proponents of it could not.

In sum, the deciding factor was the fact that, in 2012, the technology industry was more trusted by the public that the opposing coalition. This illustrates that trust matters.

Societal Trust Is Contextual Societal trust in a business is not absolute and unconditional but, rather, contextual to a particular policy position. For example, in the "World Without Free Knowledge" case of Section 2.6, not only was the coalition of Google and Wikipedia more trusted than American industry in general (refer to Figure 6.2) but, also, the profit motive was transparently behind American industry's support of SOPA/PIPA, whereas Google's opposition seemed less mercenary. Therefore, Google was more trustworthy *within the context of* the particular policy position that it took. On a different issue where, hypothetically, Google had taken a position based on a transparent profit motive, Google might have been less trusted by the public. All this is to say that trust is contextual to the issue at hand, so surveys such as Figure 6.2 must be evaluated contextually.

Also, trust is a relative judgment that is made in the comparison between two coalitions on either side of an issue. If, hypothetically, Wikipedia had supported SOPA/PIPA together with the American industry coalition, Google would have met its match in terms of trust, and perhaps even been exceeded because Wikipedia was run by a nonprofit

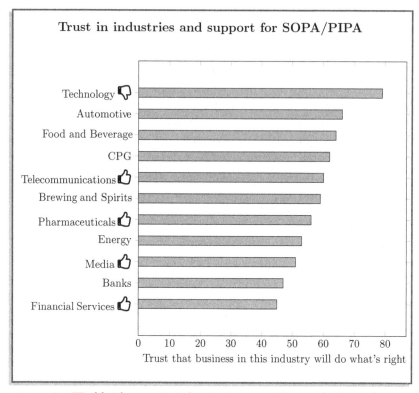

FIGURE 6.2 Worldwide trust in industries in 2012. The graph shows the average response to the question "How much do you trust businesses in each of the following industries to do what's right" (10 = not at all, 90 = a great deal). Thumbs-up symbol denotes industries that supported SOPA/PIPA, thumbs-down symbol those that opposed it. Respondents drawn from 20 countries. Source: Edelman Trust Barometer 2012.

foundation and edited by volunteers. In this hypothetical scenario, Google would have had a much tougher time mobilizing public opinion because Wikipedia would have offered the public a trusted competing narrative.

Finally, the overwhelming majority of the American public could more easily understand the direct impact on them of muzzling Internet, than the indirect, speculative, and diffuse benefit of protecting IP creation. This made it easier for the average American to trust the anti-SOPA/PIPA message.

Because trust is relative, when crafting a public opinion strategy it is important to consider whether more-highly trusted exist which can mobilize against an Agenda. This is what happened in the "World Without Free

Knowledge" case, where American industry's agenda caused opponents to mobilize that were more trusted by public opinion.

While Important, Societal Trust Is Not a Prerequisite   A public opinion campaign can be successful even if it is in support of a business or industry that is not trusted. The Pink Viagra case is an example. In the Pink Viagra case, the public opinion campaign was created against FDA scientists who are highly trusted in general (see Figure 10.3) by a business which, being pharmaceutical company, is less highly trusted in general (see Figure 6.2). And yet, the public opinion campaign was wildly successful. There are several reasons for this. The most important one is that there was no opposing coalition with a strong Motivation to call out Sprout Pharmaceutical's claims. Second, the public trusted FDA scientists to be competent in their technical judgment, but not necessarily to be immune from gender bias. Third, many members of the media/activist/regulators community were invested in the gender bias narrative. Fourth, it can be argued that the Addyi campaign was a case of "astroturf" rather than "grassroots" campaign, in that public opinion was never broadly engaged with the issue beyond being amused by the viral news items that were circulated by the media. Fifth, and related, approving Addyi would not impact the life of the average American – unlike, for example, muzzling the Internet in the "World Without Free Knowledge" case.

Narrow Trust Sometimes Suffices   Another example where *broad* societal trust is not necessary for a public opinion campaign is when public opinion is polarized. Gun regulation is such a case. A large fraction of Americans are deeply suspicious of the firearms industry – but many are not. According to an anonymous Capitol Hill staffer: "The two sides have deeply held beliefs that are in complete opposition to one another. It's like, if the NRA is effective, then that means the left groups aren't effective. But that's not true either. It's just we're at a stalemate in America. We're very divided. It's pretty much 50/50."[18]

The NRA's public opinion campaign is highly targeted at the subgroups of the population that trust the NRA. According to the same staffer: "The biggest asset the NRA has is their email list. They send something out that riles up their list. And the bigger backlash is not campaign dollars; it's the fact that your office gets overrun with people calling and writing letters and going public with the fact that you're a 'gun-grabbing liberal'."[19]

---

[18] Gutowski (2021).
[19] Gutowski (2021).

The NRA's campaign is targeted partly out of necessity, as it is essentially boycotted by mainstream media. In addition, the main goal of the campaign is to energize the NRA's base, regardless of the fact that many outside the base are put off by the NRA, and some even loathe it.

Learning Points For a public opinion strategy to be effective, it helps if the business or industry benefiting from the strategy is trusted. But, sometimes, trust is not a prerequisite for success. Also, the beneficiary business or industry need not necessarily be trusted the population as a whole, but only by the strategy's target audience.

6.7 CHECKLIST FOR A SUCCESSFUL PUBLIC OPINION STRATEGY

The above sections provide several prescriptions for building a successful public opinion strategy. These prescriptions are collected in the following framework.

Framework 5: Checklist for a successful public opinion strategy

1. Can you create a moral narrative around your product or service? (Refer to the Moral Foundations Framework at page 69.)
2. Identify the segment of public opinion that your message seeks to target. Does the target trust:
   - your industry?
   - your company?
   - your product/service?
   - your spokesperson?
3. Is there a trusted opponent that can publicly challenge your message? If so, you risk being cast as the villain!
4. Can you benefit from injecting data into the public discourse to tone down the emotional/moral content of the debate?

If the answer to item 1 is no, then a public opinion strategy is unlikely to succeed in catalyzing action. If the answer to item 1 is that a moral narrative is not desirable, then jump to item 4. Always use Framework 5 to wargame the opposing coalition's public opinion strategy.

By mentioning targeting, item 2 reminds us that moral narratives can be polarizing and that, sometimes, they don't need to resonate positively with the full spectrum of public opinion. Moreover, item 2 reminds us that trust in the industry, in the company, and even in the specific product, matters a great deal. Finally, the messenger matters, too: Figure 10.3 can be read as ranking spokespeople, from most trusted (scientists) to least trusted (CEOs and government officials).

Item 3 reminds us that trust is contextual and relative. Trust in the message can evaporate if someone more trusted, like a regulator or community activists (see Figure 10.3 again), challenges the message.

Learning Points Use the checklist provided in Framework 5 to build a successful public opinion strategy.

6.8 TAKEAWAYS FROM THIS CHAPTER

This chapter contains a number of prescriptions for businesses who are considering a public opinion strategy. Sections 6.1 and 6.2 prescribe that communication, if it is intended to activate people, must take place in the language of morality, not in the language of policy. The term morality is used here in the technical sense described in Definition 9. Framework 4 at page 69 helps make the translation. Section 6.3 acknowledges that moral language is not necessarily positive, happy, and light. This is a somewhat unsettling fact, but we must be clear-eyed about it.

The second prescription concerns decreasing the power of a moral narrative. If a business wants to decrease the resonance of a moral narrative – which is sometimes helpful – then it should inject data into the public discourse. Data and metrics tamp down on the emotional and moral content of discourse (Section 6.4). The third prescription is: Prepare for turbulence. If a public opinion strategy resonates loudly, it may well resonate differently across different people (Section 6.5). It may even be polarizing. This is a consequence of moral pluralism: Humans have different moral intuitions, that is, they load differently on the foundations of Framework 4. In some cases, this polarization can be advantageous.

Finally, Section 6.6 reminds us that a public opinion strategy is much more likely to succeed if society as a whole trusts the beneficiary business or industry. However, it is not absolutely necessary that this trust be uniform across all of society. Moreover, trust is relative and, sometimes, even a lack of trust can be overcome. These prescriptions give rise to Framework 5, which is a checklist for building a successful public opinion strategy.

7

Regulators

Regulators are different from elected officials because regulators are not motivated by electoral incentives. But then, what motivates regulators? This chapter makes the case that all regulators are motivated by a desire to uphold and increase their reputation for technical expertise. In addition, political appointees are accountable to the elected officials who have the power to remove them.

7.1 WHO ARE REGULATORS

As mentioned in Section 3.1, regulators are technical experts whose function is to inject technical knowledge into the language of the laws, to write regulations, and to ensure that the laws are properly executed and that the regulations are followed. A few top regulators are appointed by elected officials and serve at their pleasure. These are referred to as "political appointees," and they are generally replaced when the government changes. The great majority of regulators are career bureaucrats in the governmental departments or ministries. They are hired by other regulators and usually enjoy strong job security.

To become better acquainted with regulators, a good place to start is to describe a typical regulator's career.

Regulators' Career Paths Next, I will briefly describe the career paths of three regulators. Two of them are political appointees: They are the directors of the regulatory agencies featured in Minicases 4 and 6. The third regulator is the career bureaucrat who is the hero of Minicase 5. Hopefully, these descriptions will help give a sense of who regulators are.

Elizabeth Birnbaum, Director of the Minerals Management Service. The MMS was the agency tasked with collecting royalties on oil and gas production in the continental United States, as well as overseeing oil and gas production in the outer continental shelf. At the time of the *Deepwater Horizon* oil spill featured in Minicase 4, the MMS was led by Elizabeth Birnbaum. She was an attorney by training. She had earned her Juris Doctor from Harvard University, where she had been editor in chief of the *Harvard Environmental Law Review*. Her previous positions had included: lead attorney for the National Wildlife Federation (a nongovernmental organization); counsel to the House Committee on Natural Resources (i.e., working for legislators); and Associate Solicitor at the Department of Interior (a regulatory agency). She was appointed to Director of the MMS by President Obama. After leaving the MMS, she returned to the nonprofit sector working for the NGO American Rivers.

Meera Joshi, New York City Taxi and Limousine Commissioner. The TLC is the agency that regulates the taxi and the limousine industries in New York City. Around the time when Uber entered New York City, which is the subject of Minicase 6, the TLC was led by Meera Joshi. She was an attorney and had earned her Juris Doctor from the University of Pennsylvania. Her previous roles included: attorney in a prestigious law firm, and inspector general of the New York City Department of Correction. She was appointed Commissioner by Mayor de Blasio. After leaving the TLC she returned to the for-profit sector and, later, went to work for the federal government.

Frances Kelsey, pharmacologist at the Food and Drug Administration. At the time of the thalidomide crisis, which is the subject of Minicase 5, Frances Kelsey was a pharmacologist at the Food and Drug Administration, a government agency. Prior to this governmental job, she had earned her PhD in pharmacology from the University of Chicago, had been a professor there, and had practiced medicine in South Dakota.[1] Unlike the previous two regulators, Kelsey was not a political appointee.

These career paths have some features in common. First, all three regulators have a deep level of domain knowledge. Second, their careers included the private sector as well as the government. Third, their entire nongovernmental careers took place in elite institutions. Not all regulators have private sector experience in elite institutions. However, most regulators have deep domain knowledge.

Regulators' Values and Beliefs   To the extent that one's values are shaped by one's experiences and professional network, the career paths featured

---

[1] Watts (2015).

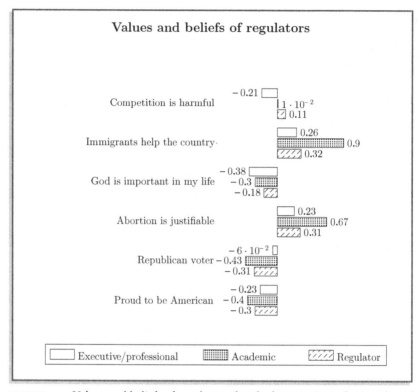

FIGURE 7.1 Values and beliefs of regulators (hatched pattern), academics (dotted pattern), and high-level executives/professionals (white color), relative to the rest of the US population. Bars represent the change in reported value/belief, measured in standard deviations, associated with the respondent being a regulator, academic, or high-level executive/professional, relative to the rest of the population. Source: World Values Survey 2017–20, elaboration by the author.

above suggest that the regulators' values and beliefs might have something in common with those of high-level executives and academics. Figure 7.1, which compares the values and beliefs of regulators with those of high-level executives, academics, and the general population, supports this hypothesis. The figure is based on data from US respondents to the World Values Survey. The horizontal bars in the figure represent the degree to which the values and beliefs expressed by regulators, academics, and high-level executives/professionals, differ from the rest of the American population. As expected, the value of all three groups depart *in the same direction* from the rest of the US population. Regulators, just as academics and high-level professionals and executives, are more likely than the rest of the population to be favorable to immigration and abortion, and less likely to be religious, nationally prideful, and politically conservative. The only value on which they split is the benefits of competition, with regulators being less trusting of competition than the average population, and executives being more trusting of it. Overall, Figure 7.1 demonstrates a remarkable alignment of values and beliefs between regulators, academics, and high-level executives and professionals.

Figure 7.1 suggests that regulators are politically more liberal than the average American. This finding is confirmed by a recent study according to which less than 30 percent of civil servants are Republican, and 50 percent are Democrats.[2] There is also considerable variation across different regulatory agencies: For example, only 5 percent of economists at the Federal Reserve, a banking regulator, are registered Republicans, and 55 percent are registered Democrats.[3] None of this is to say that government agencies are rife with partisan politics: Indeed, Spenkuch et al. (2021, p. 17) show that, outside of political appointees, regulators are not promoted more often when their personal partisan affiliation happens to align with the party of the president. However, the totality of the evidence suggests that, as concerns values and beliefs, regulators are not representative of the general population – which makes sense because they are a highly selected group.

Why the Regulators' Values and Beliefs Matter Unlike politicians, regulators are not accountable to the public: They do not have to run for election every few years.[4] Consequently, regulators do not have strong career incentives to follow the median voter's preferences. Instead, they have considerable latitude to act based on their own preferences, values, and beliefs. In addition, regulators are motivated by professional goals and constrained by professional norms. This brings us to the question: What motivates regulators? This question is addressed in the next section.

Learning Points Regulators are government employees who use their technical expertise to make the government function properly. Regulators have deep domain expertise, and their careers may include spells in the

---

[2] The rest are classified as independents: See Spenkuch et al. (2021), Figure 3.

[3] The rest are registered as independents; "not registered" not included in the percentages. Totals include employees in regional offices, who are not technically considered government employees. However, the imbalance is even starker among Board of Governors economists only. See Kuvvet (2022), totals in Table 2.

[4] This is, of course, by design: The system ensures that regulators are not subject to the pressure of public opinion.

private sector. The regulators' values and beliefs tend to align with those of academics and high-level executives and professionals.

The great majority of regulators have strong job protection and few performance-based incentives. For these regulators, the main source of incentives is the fear of losing their organization's – and their own – reputation for technical competence. A small number of top regulators serve at the pleasure of elected officials. These regulators are also motivated, to some degree, by the need to please the elected officials who can remove them.

The Cost of Losing a Reputation   The next minicase illustrates what can happen to regulators when they lose their reputation for technical competence. After an industry accident, a regulatory agency was disbanded and its director lost her government job. From a regulator's perspective, this is just about the worst case scenario.

Minicase 4: Lost reputation – the MMS and the *Deepwater Horizon* oil spill

On April 20, 2010, 5,000 feet below the sea level, a methane gas bubble formed at the base of the drill column of the *Deepwater Horizon* oil platform. The bubble of flammable gas started percolating up the drill column toward the surface at a speed of 100 feet per minute. The blowout preventer, a huge valve located on the ocean floor that was supposed to crimp the drill column and cap the well, failed. Alarms sounded on the platform, but precious time was wasted as technical failures and human errors compounded each other. Tragically, the bubble was allowed to reach the platform, where it ignited. The explosion doomed the platform and eleven oil workers.

Oil started gushing out into the Gulf of Mexico at a rate exceeding fifty thousand barrels per day.[a] As days went by, then weeks, the oil slick grew. The well continued to spill oil for months, and the oil slick grew so large that it covered most of the Gulf of Mexico. By the time the well was finally sealed, in September, the *Deepwater Horizon* accident had become the largest marine oil spill in history. Human error on the platform, as well as the mechanical failure of the blowout preventer, had combined to cause the accident.

Even as the oil was gushing out, the finger-pointing started. The Minerals Management Service (MMS), the government agency tasked with supervising offshore drilling, was immediately identified as a major culprit. It didn't help that some MMS employees had previously been found guilty of accepting improper favors from industry. In the wake of the accident, the media characterized the MMS as inadequately staffed and dependent on industry for technological know-how.[b] President Obama had harsh words for the MMS:

> Over the last decade, this agency has become emblematic of a failed philosophy that views all regulation with hostility – a philosophy that says corporations should be allowed to play by their own rules and police themselves. At this agency, industry insiders were put in charge of industry oversight. Oil companies showered regulators with gifts and favors, and were essentially allowed to conduct their own safety inspections and write their own regulations.[c]

These charges were a sharp reversal from the accolades and awards the MMS had received some years earlier by the government for its efforts to "become customer focused."[d]

This crisis was fatal for the MMS. On May 19, 2010, even as the oil kept on spilling out in the Gulf of Mexico, the MMS was disbanded, and its functions parceled out among several other government agencies. The MMS director resigned her government position.

---

[a] McNutt et al. (2012).
[b] See Priest (2010).
[c] Public Papers of the Presidents of the United States. (2010b).
[d] Carrigan (2014), p. 276. Carrigan (2014) is an excellent source for MMS's historical parabola.

The *Deepwater Horizon* accident exemplifies the regulator's nightmare. A beloved president publicly accused the MMS of being corrupt, and made it into an example of what regulators should not be. For the MMS director, this rebuke was a career-ending event: She resigned her government position and opened up a private consultancy.

A Reputation for Industry-Friendliness   Throughout the decade preceding the accident, the MMS had worked hard to develop a reputation for being cooperative with the oil and gas industry.[5] This was a strategic choice, not an accidental one: It came in response to political and social pressures for more drilling. These pressures manifested themselves through the enactment of laws that encouraged drilling,[6] and through executive action by President G. W. Bush that opened up new areas for exploration.[7] Moreover, after President Clinton had signaled a broad push for deregulation, the MMS had responded by engaging in cooperative regulation-setting with industry. Finally, between 1985 and 2010, public opinion had moved steadily in favor of economic growth and away from environmental protection.[8] Ironically, President Obama himself, less than three weeks before the *Deepwater Horizon* accident, had vouchsafed for the oil industry's safety record:

You have some environmentalists who just said "Don't drill anywhere." ... I don't agree with the notion that we shouldn't do anything. It turns out, by the way, that oil rigs today generally don't cause spills. They are technologically very advanced. Even during Katrina, the spills didn't come from the oil rigs, they came from the refineries onshore.[9]

My point is that the MMS had intentionally oriented its culture in response to pressures from political institutions and from society as large to become more industry-friendly. And yet, despite this record of docile policy positioning, or perhaps because of it, the MMS was ruthlessly axed as soon as the *Deepwater Horizon* accident happened. The MMS, it turned out, had developed the wrong kind of reputation.

An Unfair Portrayal   Several factors made it easy for the media to portray the MMS as industry lapdog, rather than watchdog. First, the MMS's budget was insufficient: The agency employed just sixty inspectors to cover nearly four thousand offshore facilities in the Gulf of Mexico. Second, it emerged that its inspections were often announced ahead of time and consisted almost exclusively of checking paperwork. Third, the

---

[5] My reading of the MMS demise follows Carrigan (2014).
[6] The Deep Water Royalty Relief Act of 1994 and the Outer Continental Shelf Deep Water Royalty Relief Act of 1995 exempted producers from paying government royalties; see Carrigan (2014), p. 275–6.
[7] Bush (2008).
[8] Carrigan (2014), p. 281.
[9] Public Papers of the Presidents of the United States (2010a).

law set negligible fines for safety violations: Over a twenty-year period, the entire industry was assessed fines amounting to just $1 million per year, relative to industry profits of $800 billion per year.[10] Fourth – and icing on the cake, from the media's perspective – was that a 2008 government report had found that MMS employees had accepted improper gifts from industry such as meals and trips. There had also been instances of improper sexual relationships between some MMS employees and industry members, though not in the division that regulated offshore production. The sum total of these factors made it easy for the media to portray the MMS as an agency that was inadequate at best, and captured by industry at worst.

Note, however, that these shortcomings were mostly caused by other parts of government, not by the MMS itself. Yes, the MMS was indeed struggling to keep up with its oversight functions, but why? Its main constraints were under-funding (only sixty inspectors) and lack of sufficient expertise (oil extraction was a high-tech business operating at ever-increasing sea depths). In addition, the government did not give it the tool to keep the industry in line (small statutory fines) and, indeed, encouraged it to cooperate with industry as described earlier. If anything, then, the truth is that the regulator's main fault had been of not being sufficiently aggressive in fighting for resources within the government.

Need for a Scapegoat Of course it is understandable that, during a crisis in which the world's media were reporting on the ongoing Gulf oil spill and giving the US government "bad press," the president would seek to deflect blame toward an obscure (to most Americans) branch of the government. After all, in a disaster of this magnitude, somebody in government must be held accountable. Moreover, the MMS was undoubtedly a media-worthy scapegoat because it had developed the wrong kind of reputation. So, two things doomed the MMS: the necessity to find a scapegoat, and the wrong kind of reputation that made the MMS a natural scapegoat in the media narrative.

Could the MMS Have Survived the Crisis? If, when the crisis hit, the MMS had had a record of fighting for resources within the government, and of using these resources aggressively to keep the oil industry accountable, the media might have adopted a different narrative: that of the underfunded but heroic agency. In this counterfactual scenario, the MMS

---

[10] Theriot (2014).

might just have survived the *Deepwater Horizon* crisis. Indeed, the crisis might even have led the government to increase the MMS's resources and statutory powers, rather than disbanding it. In my reading, therefore, the MMS could have survived the accident if its reputation had been that of industry watchdog rather than lapdog.

The Wrong Kind of Reputation Doomed the MMS   In sum, during the years leading up to the accident, the MMS had a choice about what reputation to establish. The MMS could have developed a reputation for adversarial relationship with industry, and for pro-regulation whistle-blowing and activism in the media. It did not. If it had done so, the MMS might have survived the *Deepwater Horizon* accident. The lesson from the MMS's demise is that a reputation for technical competence is important for regulators to do well, and critical for it to survive a once-in-a-century crisis such as *Deepwater Horizon*.

Learning Points   The MMS was disbanded because it had acquired the wrong kind of reputation. In general, regulatory agencies suffer when their reputation for technical competence is lost. Regulators fear losing their organization's and their own reputation for technical competence.

7.3 THE VALUE OF GAINING A REPUTATION

At the opposite end of the spectrum from the MMS, the next mini-case illustrates how a reputation for competence is gained. It describes the case of a regulatory agency that did the right thing under difficult circumstances and, as a result, was able to increase its power and prestige.

Minicase 5: Reputation gained – the FDA and Thalidomide

In the fall of 1960 Frances Kelsey, a newly hired FDA pharmacologist, was given a supposedly easy assignment: to examine and, everyone expected, approve the application for the drug Thalidomide to be marketed as a sleeping aid. Approval was thought to be a foregone conclusion because the drug had already been widely marketed in Europe without any known adverse effects.

Dr. Kelsey pored over the application materials, and she judged them incomplete. The application materials included short-term safety data on animals and humans, but no safety data on prolonged human use. Moreover, Kelsey noticed that the drug did not induce drowsiness in animals. This was an alarm bell, because it suggested that humans and animals metabolized the drug differently: Therefore, safety studies in animals may not be informative about human safety. The application materials contained several other inaccuracies. Of particular concern to Dr. Kelsey, there was no mention of safety during early pregnancy.

Dr. Kelsey requested more materials and held up the approval. This delay irked the company that had submitted the application. Its CEO suggested releasing the drug with warning labels, but Kelsey demurred. As the months went by, and without a clear path to approval, the company started lobbying the FDA:

They wrote letters and they telephoned - as often as three times a week. They telephoned my superiors and they came to see them too ... Most of the things they called me, you wouldn't print.[a]

Still, Dr. Kelsey persisted.

Eventually, disturbing evidence from Europe surfaced, indicating that the drug had severely harmed early fetal development in many babies. The first "Thalidomide baby" was born to a German employee of the chemical company that had developed Thalidomide. The baby had no ears.[b] The employee, it was later learned, had taken a sample of the drug during early gestation. Subsequently, many thousands of babies were discovered who had been born with defects caused by Thalidomide, many of them with missing or stunted limbs.

As soon as these fact started to transpire, the FDA terminated the application. Fortunately, the delay ensured that the drug was never marketed in the United States. Due to Dr. Kelsey's stubbornness, the US was spared the tragedy of Thalidomide babies. President Kennedy spoke for a grateful nation when he said:

The United States has the best and the most effective food and drug law of any country in the world, and the alert work of our food and Drug Administration, and particularly Dr. Frances Kelsey, prevented this particular drug from being distributed commercially in this country. ... We have recommended a 25 percent increase in the Food and Drug Administration staff, the largest single increase in the agency's history, and the full amount was voted today by the conferees of the Congress.[c]

In the same speech, President Kennedy advocated for increasing the regulatory powers of the FDA. Congress immediately agreed.[d] Dr. Kelsey was presented with the President's Award for Distinguished Federal Civilian Service.

[a] Seidman and Warren (2002), p. 498.
[b] Hofland (2013).
[c] Public Papers of the Presidents of the United States (1962).
[d] Carpenter (2014), p. 5256 and ff.

The point of the Thalidomide case is clear: Power and resources can flow to a government agency that is seen to be doing the right thing under difficult circumstances. Today, the FDA's regulatory powers are so extensive that FDA-regulated products represent about 20 percent of the amount spent by American consumers.[11]

Learning Points　　The government will grant power and resources to a government agency that is seen to be doing the right thing under difficult circumstances.

7.4 REGULATORS SEEK TO MAXIMIZE THEIR REPUTATION FOR TECHNICAL COMPETENCE

The general theme of the preceding sections is that regulators seek to maximize their reputation for technical expertise. This is because, in the words of Carpenter (2014): "the more legitimate, expert, and effective a regulator is perceived to be, the more likely politicians will be to create new regulations in policy areas that the regulator governs, and the more likely politicians will be to vest significant authority and resources in the regulator."[12]

The Regulators' Diverse Stakeholders　　In addition to earning greater government favor, a perception of competence helps a regulatory agency deal with its many and diverse stakeholders. If a regulatory agency is seen as competent, its employees will be more loyal; elected officials will be more likely to empower it; the businesses it regulates will be less likely to complain; the judiciary will be more deferential to the agency's expert judgment; consumer and activist groups will be less likely to attack it;

[11] Yackee (2019).
[12] Carpenter (2014), p. 54.

professional societies will be more likely to cooperate with it; and the media will support it more.[13] This enumeration indicates that a regulator must cultivate its reputation for technical competence with many diverse stakeholders.

Learning Points Regulators have many stakeholders beyond the government: its employees; the businesses it regulates; the judiciary; consumers; activist groups; professional and learned societies; and the media. Their cooperation is helpful to regulators. Regulators cultivate a reputation for competence with these diverse stakeholders.

7.5 THE REGULATORS' POLICY PREFERENCES MATTER, TOO

In Section 7.1 I discussed the regulators' personal values and beliefs. Theoretically, these personal values should not matter: Regulators should be making decisions to the best of their technical ability in order to maximize their own, and their organization's reputation for technical competence. In reality, however, the regulators' individual policy preferences probably end up skewing their technical decisions to some degree. A clever experiment illustrates this point.[14]

In the experiment, full time staff of the World Bank and of the UK's Department for International Development were asked to interpret statistical evidence regarding the effect of the minimum wage.[15] The subjects were randomly shown one of the two tables (treatments) reproduced in Table 7.1, and told that the data came from an academic study that recorded the number of localities in which, after raising (or not) the minimum wage, the income of the poorest 40 percent in the population increased. For example, the top-left entry in Scenario 1 indicates that there were 223 localities in which the minimum wage was raised and, concurrently, the income of the poorest 40 percent rose. The subjects were asked:

"Which of the following two statements is the study most consistent with?
(a) Poorest population income FALLS when the minimum wage is raised.
(b) Poorest population income RISES when the minimum wage is raised."

---

[13] Carpenter (2014), p. 50.
[14] Banuri et al. (2019).
[15] The DfID was the UK government's department responsible for administering foreign aid.

TABLE 7.1 *Alternative scenarios presented to the experimental subjects in Banuri et al. (2019).*

Experimental treatments		
Scenario 1		
	Income increased	**Income did not increase**
MinW Raised	223	75
MinW Constant	107	21
Scenario 2		
	Income increased	**Income did not increase**
MinW Constant	223	75
MinW Raised	107	21

Each scenario reports the number of localities who experienced a given change in the minimum wage level and in the income of the poorest 40 percent in the locality. Reproduced from experimental instructions in Banuri et al. (2019).

The correct answer is: (a) for subjects who were shown Scenario 1, and (b) for those who were shown Scenario 2.[16] However, the question is potentially ambiguous: indeed, Table 7.1 shows that income increased in the majority of localities, regardless of the minimum wage. So, technically, it is not wrong to say that income rose both when the minimum wage was raised, and when it wasn't. In addition, it is possible that some of the subjects may have found it difficult to go through the reasoning detailed in footnote 16 in this chapter, especially because their reward for participating in the experiment, a coffee mug, was not conditional on

---

[16] To see why this is the case, consider Scenario 1. Income increased in the majority of localities, regardless of the minimum wage. This suggests that some unmeasured confounding factor is present that tended to increase income. To parse out the causal effect of the minimum wage, we must check whether income increased *more* when the minimum wage was raised. In localities where the minimum wage was *not* raised (row 2), the number of localities in which income increased exceeds the other by a factor five, whereas in localities where the minimum wage was raised (row 1) the factor is only about three. Therefore, in Scenario 1 a minimum wage raise is associated with a smaller increase in wages. It seems, therefore, that the causal effect of the minimum wage was to depress income. The opposite is true in Scenario 2, by a similar argument.

getting the answer right. Not surprisingly, then, subjects made a lot of mistakes: Less than 50 percent of respondents answered correctly.[17]

The key finding is that the respondents' mistakes happened to correlate with their attitude toward income redistribution, which were elicited separately. Respondents who reported being more favorable to income redistribution were disproportionately more likely to mistakenly interpret Scenario 1 as suggestive that increasing the minimum wage increased the income of the poorest 40 percent. Conversely, respondents who reported being less favorable to income redistribution were disproportionately more likely to mistakenly interpret Scenario 2 as suggestive that increasing the minimum wage does not increase these same incomes. In sum, the respondents' baseline policy preferences for income redistribution colored their interpretation of the statistical evidence.

The findings of the experiment indicate that, when domain experts face a difficult technical question such as interpreting statistical evidence, their evaluations can skew toward their individual policy preferences.[18] This is a sobering conclusion, especially given the regulator's broad discretion in setting the rules of the competitive game (refer to the discussion at page 26). The experiment suggests that the typical regulator's values and desires will, to some degree, be reflected in their decision-making especially, perhaps, when the decision is a difficult one (though the experiment does not speak to the last statement directly).

Learning Points   The regulators' values and desires will, to some degree, skew their decision-making process, perhaps more so when the decision is ambiguous or difficult.

7.6 REGULATORY CAPTURE

Because regulators have great freedom of action, there is a realistic concern that they could become captured. The term "regulatory capture" refers to the notion that regulators would take actions that go against the public interest *only because* some special interests (typically, business interests) favor said actions. This section discusses regulatory capture building on the perspective laid out in Carpenter and Moss (2014).

---

[17] See Figure 1 in Banuri et al. (2019).

[18] Of course, this finding is not wholly unexpected: Judges, for example, have long been known to differ in their decisions based on their political affiliation. Still, the experiment is valuable because its subjects are not judges, but are closer to regulators, and the problem they were confronted with is more clearly a technical one compared to deciding whether a defendant is innocent or guilty.

Regulatory capture, where it exists, could be motivated by the promise, implicit or explicit, of monetary considerations – for example, the "revolving doors" phenomenon: If a regulator is friendly to firm X, then firm X may later hire the regulator at a high salary. Or, it could be an unconscious pro-industry bias, whereby regulators sincerely believe that their actions are public-spirited, but, in fact, this belief has been shaped by the industry. This might be the case in the financial industry, for example, where the very professional standards and outlook that regulators adhere to, are shaped by pro-business paradigms and principles. This is sometimes referred to as "cultural capture."[19]

How pervasive is regulatory capture by industry? Many people, including many academics, are inclined to say "a lot." There is a long and distinguished tradition, going back at least to Nobel Prize–winning economist George Stigler, that looks for empirical evidence of regulatory capture. In general, authors in this tradition seem to feel that regulatory capture is pervasive. However, this literature suffers from two measurement problems. First, this literature is based on the careful analysis of selected case studies, that is, of instances where *some* regulatory capture can be inferred from *some* agency's behavior. To my knowledge, there is no *systematic* empirical analysis of regulatory capture comparable, in breadth and scope, to the analysis discussed in Section 4.3 concerning the effect of campaign contributions on elected officials. This lack of systematic evidence is not surprising: Studying regulatory advocacy is much more difficult than studying the effect of campaign contributions. In the latter domain, both the independent variable (campaign contributions) and the dependent variables are relatively easy to measure. In the former domain, the independent variable is "arguments for or against a policy agenda" and the dependent variable is a regulatory decision: Both are difficult to measure systematically.[20] In the absence of systematic evidence on regulatory capture, we must seriously consider the possibility that the

---

[19] Kwak (2014, p. 80) identifies three mechanisms of cultural capture. "*Identity*: Regulators are more likely to adopt positions advanced by people whom they perceive as being in their in-group. *Status*: regulators are more likely to adopt positions advanced by people whom they perceive to be of higher status in social, economic, intellectual, or other terms. *Relationships*: regulators are more likely to adopt positions advanced by people who are in their social networks."

[20] To see the difficulty, recall the costly but difficult-to-measure campaign undertaken by Sprout Pharmaceutical to get the FDA to approve the drug Addyi (Section 2.7 and pages 111 and ff.). Most of Sprout's expenditures would be difficult to track down, and the outcome of Sprout's campaign, namely, an approval decision, would be difficult to code systematically across different regulatory agencies.

literature may be affected by so-called publication bias, that is, by the fact that studies that fail to detect regulatory capture may be difficult to publish in academic journals.[21] In other words, it is possible that published studies portray the exceptions (captured regulators), rather than the rule (most regulators not being captured most of the time).[22]

The second measurement problem is even more fundamental: Even within the boundaries of a case study, where a lot of contextual information is available, it can be very difficult to tease apart regulatory actions that would have been taken even in the absence of industry pressure, from actions that were taken *only because* of industry pressure. Consider, for example, the case of the Minerals Management Service (Minicase 4). As described at page 89 and ff., that ill-fated agency undertook to become industry-friendly under the combined influence of the executive, the legislature, and public opinion, over and above the influence of industry. It wasn't *only* industry pressure that caused the change in regulatory approach. Therefore, the MMS is not a clear case of regulatory capture.

All this is not to say that clear cases of regulatory capture do not exist. They do, and I consider the Pink Viagra case (Section 2.7) to be one of them. Therefore, the answer to the question, "is there regulatory capture?" is, yes, and there are many egregious cases one can point to. The relevant question for this chapter, however, is not whether there is any regulatory capture, but "how much regulatory capture is there?" Assessing, even just qualitatively, how much regulatory capture there is in the system as a whole, is a matter of judgment and experience. Two leading scholars of US regulation, Daniel Carpenter and David Moss, both of Harvard, write:

Our priors are that some amount of weak capture may well be fairly ubiquitous … When capture exists, it appears to be empirically limited rather than empirically pervasive. The picture that emerges, therefore, is quite different from the one George Stigler envisioned, in which capture by industry was virtually inevitable and complete.[23]

---

[21] See Yackee (2014) for a literature review.
[22] Public opinion may suffer from the same misperception. Most people would be ready to believe that regulatory capture is a big problem, but they may be unduly influenced by a few media-worthy cases of regulatory capture and ignore the cases, perhaps far more common, where regulators are not captured.
[23] Carpenter and Moss (2014), p. 12.

7.7 TAKEAWAYS FROM THIS CHAPTER

The MMS developed a reputation for being the lapdog rather than the watchdog of industry: This reputation doomed it during the *Deepwater Horizon* crisis. Conversely, the FDA was able to demonstrate its reputation for competence in the Thalidomide crisis and, as a result, its prestige and power grew. These examples illustrate a general principle: Regulators thrive if, and only if, they have a strong reputation for technical competence. Therefore, it makes sense for regulators to cultivate their reputation for technical competence. In addition, when technical decisions are ambiguous or difficult, regulators are liable to skew their decisions towards their own policy preferences. Regulators can, in some circumstances, be captured by industry: The extent of regulatory capture is difficult to assess empirically.

8

Advocacy Strategies with Regulators

The technical and market knowledge a business possesses – its Information, in the language of the 4Is – can be an important asset in advocating with regulators. Information can be leveraged in two ways. First, the business can share Information that is mission-relevant for the regulator. Doing so helps regulators avoid crises and, therefore, helps regulators cultivate their reputation for technical competence. This advocacy strategy is discussed in Section 8.1. Second, alternatively, the business can threaten to attack the regulator's reputation for competence. This advocacy strategy is discussed in Section 8.2. Both strategies leverage the regulators' desire to preserve and increase their reputation for technical competence.

8.1 SHARING INFORMATION

Being provided with Information allows a regulator to be more effective and, therefore, to cultivate its own reputation for technical competence. But not all information is created equal: When "soft information" is being shared, that is, when the regulator cannot interpret or verify some elements of the information being shared, sharing information requires trust.

Definition 10 (Soft versus Hard Information) *Information is **soft** when some elements of the information being shared cannot be interpreted or verified by the receiver (i.e., the regulator). Information is **hard** when the receiver can verify and interpret all elements of the information being shared.*

If a regulator does not trust the source of soft information, s/he will not trust the information itself. If the information being shared is hard information, however, the trust relationship is less important. These two scenarios are analyzed next, in turn.

Sharing Hard Information   The next minicase illustrates that being trusted by the regulator is not necessary for a firm to be able to benefit from sharing hard information.

Minicase 6: Uber sharing hard information

When Uber entered the New York City market in 2011 app-based drivers, including Uber drivers, were regulated under the for-hire vehicle (FHV) rules. FHVs were the black cars and limousines that must be hired in advance and, unlike taxis, could not be flagged while they were cruising around the city.

Before Uber's entry, taxis were required to provide the regulator with a wealth of data: pickup and drop-off location, driver identification number, fare amount, on- and off-duty time stamps, as well as GPS pings from the car's route every 30 seconds.[a] These data were used, for example, to identify taxi drivers who were caught by traffic cameras running red lights. Later, these same data would be used to ascertain that taxi drivers were making less than minimum wage. In contrast, FHVs were not required to collect any trips data. Therefore, the regulator had no visibility on the operations of FHV drivers, which numbered around 40,000 before Uber's entry.

After Uber's entry, the question arose whether Uber would be allowed to work with traditional FHV drivers. Uber was very interested in recruiting traditional FHV drivers because they constituted a large and instantly available pool of drivers. But the dispatch companies that connected passengers with FHV drivers, called "FHV Bases," were strongly opposed because Uber would be replacing their services. These companies had traditionally enjoyed a degree of monopsony, so that each FHV driver was only permitted to work with a single Base.

The taxi commissioner struck a deal with Uber. Under the deal, Uber was allowed to work with all traditional FHV drivers and, in exchange, Uber would share its trips data with the taxi commission. In addition, the commission required the Bases to start collecting and sharing trips data, which was not previously required. This deal allowed the commission to start monitoring FHV drivers and impose minimum wage regulations, as well as to limit driving hours to reduce driver fatigue and related accident risk. The taxi commissioner commented:

it really is remarkable how much the city can raise the safety standards of ... drivers and vehicles on the street, through data enforcement. This is something that I think more cities should have the ability to use.

[a] Le (2019).

This minicase is an example of a business being able to get favorable regulatory treatment by sharing data. Two observations are worth making. First, this is not a case of regulatory capture: The regulator did not, at least at a first approximation, work against the public interest by allowing Uber to work with traditional FHV drivers. In fact, it seems that the deal between Uber and the taxi commission might have been socially beneficial overall: Drivers and passengers probably benefited, even though the Bases probably lost out.

Second, the data in question was hard information, meaning that the regulator did not have to depend on Uber to interpret them. Therefore, the deal between the regulator and Uber could be struck without one side necessarily trusting the other. This was critical because little trust existed between Uber and the taxi regulators: Indeed, Uber's CEO habitually attacked the taxi regulators publicly (see page 110). Nevertheless, the deal went through because it was a mutually beneficial exchange of hard information. This is in contrast to "soft information," which is of a subjective nature such as judgments or business forecasts. Soft information can be of great value, but only if the receiver of the information trusts the sender.

The Regulators' Trust Is Key to Sharing Soft Information If a business is not trusted by the regulator, the business may not be able to benefit from sharing soft information because the information will not be trusted. In a regulated industry, this can spell disaster. The next minicase illustrates this point.

Minicase 7: CNO's inability to operate without the regulator's trust

Conseco, Inc. (an abbreviation of Consolidated National Security Corporation) was a large insurance conglomerate that did business under well-known brand names such as Colonial Penn, Washington National, and Bankers Life and Casualty Co. The company had been put together by Stephen Hilbert through acquisition of many disparate insurance businesses.[a]

In the staid world of insurance companies, Hilbert was an unusually flamboyant CEO: He had met his sixth wife while she was working as an exotic dancer, he had paid himself $172 million as the CEO of Conseco and, in addition, given himself loans from the company exceeding $160 million. In 2002, Conseco filed for Chapter 11 bankruptcy – it was the third largest US bankruptcy at the time.

Five years later, the company that emerged from bankruptcy had a new CEO and a new name, CNO Financial. The new company, however, was experiencing difficulties with its Long Term Care (LTC) policies. These policies had been issued in the early 1980s by businesses that were later absorbed into Conseco. These businesses were now consolidated in a subsidiary called CSHI, which was bleeding money. In the preceding five years Conseco had contributed $1 billion in capital into CSHI and had received no dividends.

CSHI's financial problems were partly systemic to the industry. The LTC market's "original sin" dated back to the 1980s, when policies had been underwritten that soon became massively underpriced. The underpricing became apparent when massive medical-cost inflation occurred, which caused the contractually stipulated monthly premiums to become insufficient to cover the claims.

In addition to systemic problems, CSHI had its own specific problems due to the fragmented nature of the contracts it held. Because the company had grown by acquisition, its portfolio contained very disparate contracts; this made it difficult for the company to correctly service each contract. This fragmentation increased administrative costs and, in addition, made CNO prone to mistakenly deny coverage in some instances, a fact that caused negative publicity in the media.

While other companies in the LTC market were able to successfully petition the insurance regulators for premium increases, CSHI's petitions were frequently rejected. Regulators informally told the CEO that CSHI might get premium increases, but it would never be allowed to pay a dividend back to CNO.

The regulators' ill-will against the new company was largely due to the old company's checkered history. Even though the new CEO was financially conservative and the new company had not been involved in any malfeasance, in the regulators' eyes the new company was tainted.

Given the scale of the losses caused by CSHI's inability to obtain premium increases, the new CEO faced a number of unappealing options.

1. **Continue to operate CSHI.** That would mean continuing to lose $200 million per year with no foreseeable prospect of improvement.
2. **Sell CSHI.** But who would buy it?
3. **Declare CSHI bankrupt.** Technically that was feasible, but the insurance regulators would be furious because bankruptcy would nullify the current policyholders' contracts, which would hurt the policyholders. Since CNO was engaged in a long term relationship with the regulators, their displeasure over CSHI could weaken CNO's future regulatory position in other important markets.
4. **Spin CSHI off as separate company.** The spin-off company would face the same problems that CNO was facing and, likely, end up bankrupt – see above point.
5. **Mutualize CSHI.** Mutualization would mean "selling" the company to the policy holders. Under this arrangement, the policy holders would collectively own CSHI, similar to a cooperative.

None of these options was appealing, but only one had the advantage of restoring the regulator's trust: This was the option to mutualize. Mutualization would effectively turn the company into a nonprofit. Then, regulators would find it much more palatable to grant the company the premium increases it needed to survive.

In the end, CSHI was mutualized and changed its name to SHIP. The regulators required CNO to give SHIP a "dowry" of $175 million as a parting subsidy. SHIP elected a board of respected trustees including a former US Surgeon General.

---

[a] This case is based on Persico and Prieur (2017).

The CNO case illustrates the difficulty of conveying soft information in the absence of trust. To petition for a premium increase, the company was required to provide evidence that it could not profitably service its existing contracts. That sort of financial information was manipulable by CNO, hence it was "soft information." Given CNO's history, the regulators felt they could not trust the company to be truthful in its representations.

Furthermore, even if insurance regulators had trusted the new management, they would have wanted to look tough in their dealings with CNO because the old company, Conseco, had diminished the regulators' reputation for technical competence by going bankrupt. Being tough on the new company represented a way for the regulators to repair their own reputation.

Both problems were solved by mutualizing CSHI. The new mutualized spin-off was no longer a scapegoat for insurance regulators because CNO was no longer the owner. Indeed, the mutualization could be portrayed as a success for the regulators because they forced CNO to pay a big dowry to the mutualized company.

The CNO case is instructive in that the regulators' lack of trust was so radical, that CNO simply could not operate in a highly regulated market such as the LTC market, where profit margins depended entirely on the regulators' good will. CNO's reputation with the regulators was so bad that it had to exit the LTC market.

The Benefits of Sharing Soft Information   When regulators trust, or at least do not mistrust a company, sharing soft information can yield great benefits. This is illustrated in the next minicase, which is connected with the *Deepwater Horizon* accident (refer back to page 88).

Minicase 8: Trust meets informational advantage – the blowout preventer

In the very first days of the *Deepwater Horizon* spill, MMS employees urgently reached out to a leading energy technology company and asked for permission to visit their facilities. MMS wanted to discuss whether the failed blowout preventer, which was presently lying uselessly on the ocean floor, could somehow be revived and used to stop the ongoing oil spill. The technology company agreed to the visit.

Crucial background information: The technology company manufactured blowout preventers, but not the one that had caused the *Deepwater Horizon* accident. Also, the company had a sterling reputation for technical knowledge.

When the MMS regulators showed up at the company's facilities it became clear, much to the technology company's surprise, that the regulators had very limited knowledge of what a blowout preventer even looked like. At that moment, the technology company realized that it could have authoritatively advocated for the MMS to mandate any amount of new safety technology for underwater oil extraction, no matter how expensive. Being a supplier of this technology, the company could have benefited considerably from any such mandate.

In the event, the technology company behaved ethically and did not mislead the regulators into mandating useless but expensive safety technology. But it could have.

The blowout preventer minicase shows that, as long as a business is not mistrusted by regulators, sharing soft information can be productive both for the business and for the regulators. In the minicase, the regulators' need for information was so great and so urgent, that the company could have potentially influenced regulations by sharing soft information. Let me emphasize again: For this to work, it is absolutely necessary that the company not be mistrusted by the regulators. If the company had had a less sterling reputation, or if its products had been involved in the *Deepwater Horizon* accident, the visit described in Minicase 8 would not have happened and the opportunity to influence regulation would not have arisen.

Earning Trust by Sharing Information   The next minicase shows how Microsoft was able to earn trust by sharing information with legislators and regulators, and by behaving responsibly over a prolonged time period. The minicase also illustrates how Microsoft capitalized on that trust in a tricky situation.

Minicase 9: Microsoft earns trust by sharing information

In 2020, the House of Representative's antitrust subcommittee spent hours grilling the CEOs of some of the largest US information technology companies. In the hot seat were: Alphabet

(Google), Amazon, Apple, and Facebook. The tone was hostile. The committee chairman started out the session by declaring:

Our founders would not bow before a king. Nor should we bow before the emperors of the online economy.

The questions for Alphabet concerned online search dominance, its operations in China, its reluctance to work with the US military, and its treatment of politically conservative speech. The questions for Amazon concerned the treatment of independent sellers on its platform. The questions for Apple concerned the openness of its App Store. The questions for Facebook concerned anti-competitive acquisition practices and its treatment of politically conservative speech.[a]

Conspicuously absent was Microsoft: The company had not been asked to testify. Instead, Microsoft president Brad Smith had prepared the lawmakers for the hearing. Smith's advice to the lawmakers was understood by some of them as: "asking these CEOs tough questions is a good thing."[b] Behind the scenes, Microsoft was, in effect, orchestrating the prosecution.

How did Microsoft land the enviable role of prosecuting its competitors? By cooperating with legislators and regulators. Over the years, Microsoft had made senior employees and technical staff available to brief legislators and regulators on technology policy, such as responding to cyberattacks or sharing data across countries. Furthermore, Microsoft had withdrawn from membership in trade associations that lobbied on behalf of the tech industry. Finally, Microsoft had quietly made available its secure collaboration environment "Microsoft 365 for Campaigns" to all US federal and state political campaigns and parties, for the nominal price of $5 per month.[c]

According to a lobbyist not paid by Microsoft,

Microsoft has pursued a strategy of trying to position itself apart from Big Tech and as the most responsible player.[d]

[a] Tracy (2020).
[b] Tilley and Tracy (2022).
[c] See https://m365forcampaigns.microsoft.com/en-us/.
[d] Tilley and Tracy (2022).

This minicase illustrates that sharing information can be more than an advocacy strategy aimed at implementing an Agenda: It can help increase trust. Of course, it is important for any company that achieves a position of trust and informational advantage to behave ethically, and not to take advantage of its position. This must be a core principle of SBM.

Advocacy through Information-Sharing This section has highlighted several principles that can help a business to advocate by sharing information. These principles are summarized in Framework 6.

Framework 6: Advocacy through Information-Sharing

1. Sharing information can help a business to advocate for a preferred regulatory standard (Minicases 6 and 8) and to build trust with the regulator (Minicase 9).
2. Information can be hard, that is, verifiable by the regulator (often, data); or soft, that is, nonverifiable (such as opinion/advice).
3. Soft information is not credible without trust (Minicase 7), but hard information can be (Minicase 6).
4. Information must be shared ethically to avoid even the appearance of regulatory capture.

The exchange of information between a business and its regulators can take place in many ways. Regulators may reach out and request information, as happened in the blowout preventer visit (Minicase 8). Businesses may reach out to the regulators, perhaps through a lobbyist. And, finally, businesses may meet with regulators at industry meetings.

Learning Points Regulators need information to be seen as competent by their stakeholders (for a list of them, refer to page 94). A business has information about customers, technology, and so on that can help them do that. This information represents a source of power for business. Therefore, a business or industry can benefit by sharing information with regulators.

8.2 THREATENING THE REGULATOR'S REPUTATION

So far, I have discussed information-sharing strategies that help the regulator increase its reputation for technical competence. A different, and more aggressive strategy, is to threaten the regulator's reputation. This is not difficult to do: Many companies are in a position to threaten the regulator's motives, or its competence. But it may not be wise to do so.

Uber's Attacks Uber's CEO Travis Kalanick regularly attacked taxi regulators publicly. For example, speaking at a business conference in 2012, Kalanick mused about his experience with regulators and listed the following three features of the regulatory mindset:

- "Cronyism. They get a Stockholm Syndrome with the folks they regulate.... One even told me that they view themselves as customer support for the taxi and livery companies.
- "If they don't have rules, they feel it is illegal.
- "They are incredibly sensitive to what's the public view, the optics rather than the reality."[1]

Clearly, these words are designed to attack the taxi regulators' reputation for competence. Interestingly, Kalanick refrained from ever attacking Chinese regulators even though they treated Uber much worse than US-based regulators (see page 154). This difference in Kalanick's public stance toward regulators in different countries suggests that his attacks on US-based regulators were not emotional outbursts but, rather, part of an intentional strategy.

NRA's Attacks In light of the NRA's rhetorical posture described in Minicase 3, it is not surprising that the NRA has attacked the credibility of its regulator. Back in 1995, the president of the NRA referred to agents of the Bureau of Alcohol, Tobacco and Firearms (ATF), its regulator, as "jack-booted government thugs." He also said that the goal of the ATF was to "take away our constitutional rights, break in our doors, seize our guns, destroy our property and even injure or kill us ... if you have a badge, you have the government's go-ahead to harass, intimidate, even murder law-abiding citizens."[2]

This aggressive rhetoric has persisted over the years. In 2022, materials published on the NRA's Institute for Legislative Action website read:

Recently, the ATF – under the direction of Joe Biden and Merrick Garland – has been on a tear of upsetting settled understandings and changing enforcement policies.... Even though the words of statutes and – in some cases, regulations – haven't changed, things that were understood to be legal are suddenly declared illegal.... Sometimes the actions have even been expressly approved by ATF's own prior statements or rulings.[3]

---

[1] Lunden (2012).
[2] Quoted from Keil (1995) and Mintz (1995).
[3] NRA-ILA (2022).

These attacks questioned the motives of the ATF. As regards the ATF's competence, a key theme of the NRA's attack on the ATF was that gun regulations don't work because only law-abiding citizens are constrained by them. The implication was that the ATF goes about its business in the wrong way. The effect of these attacks has been to hamper ATF's activity. According to Vizzard (1995): "The NRA's strategy of seeking controversy has fostered an environment that discourages the bureaucracy from seeking solutions through experimentation in implementation or modification of existing law."

Pharma's Attacks   Another example of business attacking a regulator has been provided in Minicase 5, which describes how, after the pharmacologist Frances Kelsey help up the approval of the drug Thalidomide, the company seeking approval attacked Kelsey's reputation for competence with her superiors. In her own words: "They wrote letters and they telephoned - as often as three times a week. They telephoned my superiors and they came to see them too. . . . Most of the things they called me, you wouldn't print."[4]

Such an aggressive strategy is rarely advisable because, in the long run, the regulator has the statutory powers to get back at the company. However, in some cases this strategy can be spectacularly successful in the short run. The Pink Viagra case in Section 2.7 provides an example of short-term success.

Sprout's Multipronged Attack   In the Pink Viagra case, Sprout Pharmaceutical's strategy threatened the regulator's (in that case, the FDA's) reputation by implying that any reluctance to approve Addyi reflected gender bias. Of course, such a bias would mean that the FDA did not follow impartial scientific standards. The presence of gender bias among FDA scientists seemed plausible to some, so the threat to the FDA's reputation was real. This threat caused the FDA to crumble under the pressure.

In order to create a credible threat, Sprout operated on several complementary fronts. First, Sprout Pharmaceutical was able to leverage a preexisting industry play: Well before Flibanserin was owned by Sprout, in the early days of the Viagra blockbuster drug for men, the pharmaceutical industry had been working on so-called "disease branding," that is, on the creation of a disease that does not exist in order to sell a drug that exists. Back then, the pharmaceutical companies were trying to get

---

4 Seidman and Warren (2002), p. 498.

FDA approval for testosterone-based treatments for women's libido. In the 2003 article "The Making of a Disease: Female Sexual Dysfunction," published in the *British Medical Journal*, it was argued that:

companies first require a clearly defined medical diagnosis with measurable characteristics to facilitate credible clinical trials. Over the past six years [i.e., starting in 1997] the pharmaceutical industry has funded, and its representatives have in some cases attended, a series of meetings to come up with just such a definition [of female sexual dysfunction].[5]

The effort to define a new sexual dysfunction disease was noticed and called out in several articles published in prestigious medical journals such as the *British Medical Journal* and *PLos Medicine*. The articles had titles such as "Female Sexual Dysfunction: A Case Study of Disease Mongering and Activist Resistance."[6] Just a few months before Addyi was approved by the FDA, an article published in the *Journal of Medical Ethics* under the title "Hypoactive Sexual Desire Disorder: Inventing a Disease to Sell Low Libido" called out Sprout Pharmaceutical's tactic of funding continuing education modules for doctors in which: "hypoactive sexual desire disorder was cast as a common, underdiagnosed problem that has a profound adverse effect on quality of life and the lack of treatments for women's sexual problems was presented as an urgent unmet need."[7]

In sum, on the disease branding front, Sprout had picked up where others in the pharmaceutical industry had left off. On the advocacy front, according to Hogenmiller et al (2017):

The campaign hired two feminists: a former director of the FDA Office of Women's Health, and the former president of the Women's Research and Education Institute – both well-known to women's groups. Even the Score recruited and paid consumer advocacy groups to pressure the FDA into approving Flibanserin for Hypoactive Sexual Desire Disorder – a condition previously created by industry to sell another drug.

These hires boosted the campaign's credibility within the women's health community. And, finally, there was the public opinion campaign which has been discussed in Section 2.7.

The number of fronts on which Sprout acted suggests that these fronts were complementary. In other words, all three components of the strategy – influencing the medical science, enlisting trusted advocates in the

---

[5] Moynihan (2003).
[6] Meixel et al. (2015).
[7] Meixel et al. (2015).

feminist community, and the public opinion campaign – were all required in order to influence the FDA scientists. This observation suggests that the FDA scientists were susceptible to influence from multiple sources: from the medical community, from social activist groups, and from mass media. This observation squares with Travis Kalanick's comment about regulators: "They are incredibly sensitive to what's the public view, the optics rather than the reality."[8] This observation also squares with the fact that regulators have many diverse stakeholders: refer back to page 94. I will return to this point in the next section.

Advocating by Threatening the Regulator's Reputation This section has illustrated several important common features in the cases where businesses benefited from attacking their regulators' competence. These regularities are summarized in the following framework.

Framework 7: Advocating by threatening the regulator's reputation

- Many companies and industries are in a position to threaten the regulator's motives, or its competence.
- The attack may take the form of a narrative that is different from the regulator's (e.g., the NRA's argument that gun laws constrain law-abiding citizens only)
- ... and even of directly attacking the regulator's credibility (e.g., Pharma's attack on Kelsey, or Sprout's attack on the FDA)
- A business should not attack if it expects to interact with the regulator in the future – unless the issue is existential
- A business should not attack unless the goal of the business is ethically defensible (arguably, this might be the case in Uber's case, for example).

Learning Points Regulators need to be seen as competent by multiple stakeholders (refer to page 94). Threatening this reputation for competence can be advantageous for business. However, this strategy can, and should, be used sparingly as recommended in Framework 7.

---

[8] Quoted at page 110.

8.3 TAKEAWAYS FROM THIS CHAPTER

There can be great advantage in sharing information that the regulator needs. Being trusted by the regulator is not necessary in order to benefit from sharing hard information. To benefit from sharing soft information, however, trust is necessary. Trust is not required if the strategy is to attack the regulator's reputation – recall the Pink Viagra case. However, attacking the regulator's reputation should not be done unless the goal is ethically defensible. Moreover, attack is rarely a wise strategy because the regulator is usually in a position to hurt the company in the future.

9

Preemption

Sometimes, it is possible for an industry to preempt government regulation by mitigating the societal concerns that prompt the government to intervene. This is desirable when government intervention is likely to be clumsy. Executing However, executing preemption is difficult. The challenge lies in the absence of enforcement power: Not every industry player, and sometimes no single industry player, necessarily has an incentive to do what is desirable for the industry as a whole. And, by construction, there is no Institution with which has the statutory power to impose change. This chapter studies two general settings in which this challenge exists and, nevertheless, despite this challenge being present, the industry is able to preempt clumsy government intervention.

The key ideas are illustrated through events that took place in the movie industry. The movie industry preempted government regulation of explicit content twice: first in the 1930s (refer back to Section 2.3), then in the 1960s when the movie rating system was devised (more in Section 9.2). The difference between these two instances is instructive, and it will be used to highlight a general bifurcation in the kind of problems that preemption can address. Accordingly, this chapter will be divided into two sections, each dealing with a distinctive kind of setting where preemption can help and the specific strategy required in that setting. The chapter will also discuss the experience of the telemarketing and e-cigarette industries.

The goal of this chapter is not to teach how to avoid regulation; rather, it is to teach how an industry can put in place a regulation that achieves the government's goals with the least amount of burden on the industry and consumers.

9.1 SELF-REGULATION

What is self-regulation? In this book, I use the word self-regulation in a specific sense. Here is my definition.

Definition 11 (Self-Regulation)   *A firm self-regulates if it voluntarily adheres to a costly standard that is not legally mandated.*

For example, if featuring a risqué scene would make a movie more popular, cutting the scene in order to uphold traditional values represents a form of self-regulation for a film production company. Similarly, not producing popular fruit-flavored e-cigarettes in order to prevent teen addiction to nicotine is a form of self-regulation for a vaping company. In Definition 11, "voluntarily" means "in the absence of governmental coercion." Self-regulation, in this definition, means going above and beyond what the law requires. Henceforth, I will refer to the voluntary adherence to a costly standard as "self-restraint." Therefore, self-regulation in Definition 11 is the same as exercising self-restraint.

Self-regulation is called for when an industry suffers from bad public perception caused by industry members pushing ethical boundaries in the pursuit of short-term profit. If firms in the industry could exercise self-restraint, public perception would improve. Absent self-restraint, however, public perception is bad and the industry runs the risk of onerous government regulation. Self-regulation aims to preempt onerous government regulation by ensuring that firms in an industry behave in a way that meets societal expectations and, also, makes business sense.

Note that if the industry is composed of a single firm, that is, it is monopolistic, we would expect the firm to have little difficulty in adopting the optimal level of self-régulation. If the industry is composed of many firms, however, it may be more difficult for these firms individually to adopt a sufficient level of self-regulation. I will revisit this point in Theorem 1 below.

Successful Self-Regulation: Hays Code   Recall the movie industry's problem in the 1920s (refer to Section 2.3): The industry had a great product, but it was under attack by high-minded reformers with a big media presence. These reformers used the media outlets they controlled, including magazines and church pulpits, to call out the movie industry. They painted the movies as a "sin product" and sought to control the industry's license to operate. At the time, the industry was already clumsily regulated by local censors, and the reformers were pressing for a possibly even less friendly form of regulation: a federal board of censorship. Faced with this risk and with growing attacks on their reputation, the Hollywood studios self-regulated by creating a standard, the Hays Code, which listed identified bright-line rules defining what it meant for a movie to be wholesome. Consistent with Definition 11, adhering to this standard was costly for each individual studio: Short-term profits were forgone because any individual studio could have produced risqué content and attracted more than its fair share of moviegoers. Self-regulation was successful in that it made it possible to successfully push back on, and eventually to eliminate censorship.

Failure to Self-Regulate: Vaping Industry Self-regulation failed in the vaping industry, as discussed in Section 2.5. Vaping had the potential to do much good for society: It was less harmful than smoking cigarettes and, if cigarette smokers would switch to vaping, many lung cancer deaths could be prevented. However, vaping was addictive. FDA regulators had initially allowed the industry to develop with little regulation. But the industry lost credibility by aggressively marketing fruit-flavored products and even cannabis-based products to minors. As a result, youth vaping skyrocketed. Regulators felt betrayed and came down hard on the industry. Vaping became highly regulated in the United States. This case illustrates how the failure to self-regulate triggered onerous government regulations.

Failure to Self-Regulate: Telemarketing Industry Outbound telemarketing is the practice of cold-calling peoples' phones at all hours of the day to pitch products or services. The US outbound telemarketing industry failed to self-regulate, as illustrated in the next minicase.

Minicase 10: The demise of outbound telemarketing

In 1991, outbound telemarketers were calling 18 million Americans daily. By 2002, that number had jumped to 104 million.[a] This growth indicates that outbound telemarketing was very profitable and, perhaps, that some Americans found value in some of the calls, some of the time.

But, also, many million Americans found these calls annoying. The risk for the industry was that millions of voters would demand the end of telemarketing, or at least a tight regulation of telemarketing practices. This risk was not fully internalized by each individual telemarketing company. Therefore, each company tended to call too much, too often.

Eventually, the frustration of millions of Americans boiled over. In 2003, the federal government created a "do-not-call list" on which individuals could register their phone numbers; registration ensured that no telemarketer could call them. These lists proved very popular: 100 million Americans signed up for the do-not-call list within the first two years. Effectively, the do-not-call list ended the outbound telemarketing industry.

a Hurst (2008).

This minicase illustrates how the inability to self-regulate doomed the telemarketing industry.

Self-Regulation Is Underprovided   Absent an enforcement mechanism, self-regulation will necessarily be below the industry-efficient level. This is because the costs of firm i's self-restraint are borne entirely by firm i itself in the form of reduced profits. The benefits of firm i's self-restraint, in contrast, are enjoyed by all the firms in the industry in the form of reduced probability of government regulation. Therefore, firm i does not internalize the full benefits of its own self-restraint. This mismatch results in insufficient self-restraint.

For example, in Minicase 10, each individual telemarketing firm had a profit motive to call consumers early and often. This pattern of behavior would get consumers annoyed and, thus, increase the probability of regulatory intervention. But the cost of any new regulatory intervention would not fall solely on the firm in question: Much of it would fall on other firms in the industry. Therefore, an individual telemarketing firm would internalize the full benefits of its annoying behavior (through profits), but it would externalize the majority of the regulatory costs (risk of regulation, which was borne by the entire industry). This mismatch means that telemarketing firms only partially internalized the industry-level benefits of restraint.

Put more abstractly, the argument is that self-restraint is an industry-level public good. Therefore, firm i's private incentives are to underprovide self-restraint relative to the industry-level optimum (the industry-level optimum is the level of firm i's self-restraint that equates the marginal cost of self-restraint with its industry-level benefit). In sum, we can expect self-regulation to be less than the level that is optimal for the industry as a whole. This underprovision is more pronounced if there are more firms in the industry. If the industry is made up of a single firm, we expect self-regulation to achieve its efficient level.

This discussion is summarized in the following theorem.

Theorem 1 (Self-Restraint Is Underprovided) *Self-restraint, i.e., voluntary adherence to a costly standard, is an industry-level public good. Therefore, it is underprovided unless there is only one firm in the industry. The greater the number of firms in an industry, the more self-restraint is underprovided relative to the industry-level optimum.*

Self-enforcement Is the Limiting Factor Obviously, for an industry that is threatened by onerous government regulation, self-regulation is an appealing alternative to clumsy government intervention. The main factor that limits an industry's ability to self-regulate is lack of enforcement power. Theorem 1 suggests that self-regulation is underprovided and so some form of enforcement is required to achieve the level of self-regulation that is optimal for the industry. However, by definition, the power of government is not available to punish firms that do not adhere to the high standard of conduct that is optimal for the entire industry. Enforcement, therefore, must be supplied by the industry itself. This is challenging because firms may not want to, or may not be able to punish each other for failing to adhere to the costly standard.

Market Fundamentals That Promote Self-Enforcement Self-enforcement is the limiting factor for successful self-regulation. The next framework lists the market fundamentals that promote self-enforcement. Underlying the following framework is a standard of conduct that industry players agree to follow in principle, but from which they may deviate in practice.

> **Framework 8: Market fundamentals that promote self-enforcement**
>
> 1. High industry profits under self-regulation
> 2. Threat of government regulation is severe
> 3. Gains from deviating are small
> 4. Industry members expect to interact repeatedly in the future
> 5. Detecting deviations is easy
> 6. Sanctioning deviators is easy
> 7. Corporate leadership is not short-termist

In this framework, the term "deviation" refers to abandoning self-restraint, i.e., to a failure to adhere to the standard of conduct. Where

---

The self-regulation dilemma

| | **Firm 2** | |
Firm 1	self-restraint	no self-restraint
self-restraint	4,4	1,5
no self-restraint	5,1	2,2

FIGURE 9.1 The self-regulation dilemma. Individually, each firm benefits from exercising no self-restraint, but this behavior causes a high likelihood of clumsy government intervention and, therefore, of value destruction.

does Framework 8 come from? I discuss the conceptual foundations of this framework next.

Technical Aside: Game-Theoretic Foundations of Framework 8   Framework 8 originates from game theory. To trace the connection with game theory, think of self-enforcement as voluntary cooperation in a prisoner's dilemma played among industry members. Figure 9.1 illustrates this game in the case of an industry with two firms. If both firms exercise self-restraint, payoffs are high for both firms because the threat of government intervention is remote. If firm 1 exercises self-restraint but firm 2 doesn't, firm 2 is able to steal business from firm 1; in addition, the threat of government intervention increases, hence total industry payoffs decrease (they equal $5 + 1 = 6$, which is less than $4 + 4 = 8$), even though firm 2 is better off than before. Finally, if neither firm exercises self-restraint, clumsy government intervention is highly likely and so payoffs are very low.

The first three items in Framework 8 can be interpreted as features of the payoff matrix in Figure 9.1. The first item says that if all the firms in the industry exercise self-restraint, that is, if the industry is able to achieve self-enforcement, then the firms' payoffs are high. The second item says that if no firm exercises self-restraint, the firms' payoffs are low. If that is the case, collective self-restraint is very valuable for the industry. And, if the individual gains from deviation are small (third factor), it might be possible to tweak the game so as to restore self-enforcement.

At this point, the reader who is familiar with game theory might question whether thinking about self-enforcement as a prisoner's dilemma is really fruitful, since the only Nash equilibrium in a prisoner's dilemma is for all players to defect. Sadly, game theory seems to predict that self-enforcement can never arise in equilibrium. However, not all is lost. What is needed is a tweak to change the game from a prisoner's dilemma to something else that is more conducive to cooperation. That tweak is provided by *repetition* (fourth factor). If players play a *repeated* prisoner's dilemma, meaning, in our case, that industry members interact repeatedly over time, then after an industry member defects there is an opportunity to punish it.

The possibility of punishing defectors creates cooperative equilibria in repeated prisoner's dilemmas. These equilibria work as follows. Every firm starts out by cooperating – in our case, adopting self-restraint – and continues to do so as long as everyone has cooperated in the past. As soon as anyone has failed to cooperate in the past, every firm abandons self-restraint forever. In this equilibrium, no firm ever defects because they know that any defection triggers a permanent switch to a lower-payoff state.

In order for the above cooperative equilibrium to be played, it must be possible to detect and punish deviators. Factors five and six speak to the ability of industry members to detect and punish firms that fail to self-restrain. Moreover, in order for firms to be willing to play the cooperative equilibrium, they must be patient enough that the net present loss from punishing each other forever (future lost profits) outweighs the immediate gain from deviating. This requires that firms be patient. Factor seven speaks to the propensity of possible defectors to trade off a short-term gain against a long-term loss.

In sum, the market fundamentals that promote self-enforcement come from the mathematical theory of repeated games. They are the same fundamentals that promote cartel formation, for example. Thus, as a rule of thumb, industries that are prone to cartelization are also expected to be able to self-regulate.

Applying Framework 8   What market fundamentals enabled the movie industry to self-regulate through the Hays code? Conversely, why did the vaping and telemarketing industries fail to self-regulate? Framework 8 can help answer these questions.

Applying Framework 8 to the Movie Industry   In the case of the movie industry of Section 2.3, all the items in Framework 8 point to the feasibility of strong self-regulation. The industry could make strong profits even while adhering to the Hays Code. The threat of government regulation was severe, and even the status quo was bad, with fragmented and arbitrary local censorship. Detecting firms that deviated from the Hays Code was easy because movies are publicly observable. Therefore, the industry was in a position to enforce adherence to the Hays Code.

Further supporting the notion that the Hays Code was enforceable, deviators could be punished due to the oligopolistic and vertically integrated nature of the industry. The Big Five studios (Warner Bros, Paramount, RKO, MGM, Fox Film) together produced more than 90 percent of movies in America, distributed each other's films both nationally and internationally, and owned the movie theaters (about 50 percent of the seating capacity in most first-run houses in major US cities). This industry structure permitted any single "deviator" studio that produced a film in violation of the Hays Code to be punished by the other four studios. This punishment could be meted out by not showing the offending movie in their theaters and by not distributing it elsewhere.

Whether the gains from deviating were small or large is arguable. In my estimation they were small because, if a major studio had "gone rogue" and ignored the Hays Code altogether, it would have been detected quickly and would have triggered a collective response. If this is the case, then the gains from deviating are relatively small. Finally, it is worth noting that the movie studios were owned by the same owners for long periods of time, suggesting that these owners had a long-term outlook and would not have risked destroying long-term industry cooperation for short-term gain.

Because the movie industry in the 1930s checked so many items in Framework 8, we should not be surprised that the movie industry was able to self-regulate.

Applying Framework 8 to the Vaping Industry   By contrast, the vaping industry in Section 2.5 failed to check many of the items in Framework 8. First, to the extent that self-regulation meant not selling to youths, profits under self-regulation would be relatively low. This feature reduced the appeal of self-enforcement. Second, detecting deviators, that is, firms that aggressively marketed to youths, was difficult because of the industry structure, with many fly-by-night producers that produced e-liquids, and also because marketing to youth was not always overt, especially over the internet. Third, sanctioning deviators may not have been possible for vaping firms – unlike for the Hollywood studios. Fourth, the gains from deviating were huge because, in a counterfactual world where all firms chose not to sell fruit flavors or cannabis, the only company selling flavored or cannabis e-liquids could grow its market share very fast. Fifth, the majority owner of leading vaping company JUUL was Altria (formerly Philip Morris), a public company with short-term profit pressures.

Because the vaping industry did not check many items in Framework 8, it makes sense that the industry was unable to self-regulate.

Applying Framework 8 to the Telemarketing Industry Similarly, the outbound telemarketing industry did not check many of the items in Framework 8. In particular, the industry was highly competitive so profits, whether in the regulated or unregulated scenario, were low. Second, detecting deviators would be extremely difficult and punishing them nearly impossible. Because the telemarketing industry did not check many items in Framework 8, it makes sense that the industry was unable to self-regulate.

Government as a Facilitator The government can, if it so chooses, boost an industry's ability to self-enforce by delegating to the industry the power to revoke its own members' license to operate. The government does this for licensed professions. Lawyers and doctors, for example, are accredited by licensing boards. The government forbids these practitioners from operating unless they are licensed. In this way, the government effectively delegates to the industry the power to license its own individual practitioners. In turn, the licensing boards are expected to use their powers to punish practitioners who deviate from professional norms of conduct. Going back to Definition 11, the licensing boards are effectively made into regulatory agencies, invested by the government with the statutory power to punish deviators. The reason why the government delegates this power rather than exercising it directly is that the government does not have the expertise to judge when a practitioner deviates from professional norms.

Applicability of Framework 8 to Generic Coalition Formation Framework 8 is presented as a list of factors that facilitate industry coordination on the issue of preempting government intervention. Coordination was previously discussed in Section 5.2 within a different context: generic coalition formation. Within that context, Framework 8 can serve as a list of factors that make it easier for a generic coalition to coordinate on any Issue. A technical difference is that, in this Section 9.1, agents coordinate to undertake a costly action whereas, in Section 5.2, agents coordinate to enthusiastically communicate the same message. But this difference is inconsequential, because, just like a costly action, communication has material consequences in Section 5.2, too. Also, nothing in

Framework 8 restricts its applicability to a single industry: The factors listed in the framework can be checked for any coalition, whether or not its members are part of the same industry. Therefore, Framework 8 can be understood as a list of factors that make it easier for a generic coalition to coordinate on any Issue.

Learning Points   Self-regulation means going above and beyond what the law requires of the firm. Self-regulation is expedient when an industry suffers from bad public perception that is caused by industry members pushing ethical boundaries in the pursuit of short-term profit. The limiting factor in an industry's ability to self-regulate is self-enforcement. Framework 8 lists the factors that promote self-enforcement, and therefore make it easier for the industry to self-regulate. The government can boost an industry's ability to self-regulate by delegating to the industry the power to revoke its members' license to operate.

9.2 VOLUNTARY CERTIFICATION

In this book, I use the word voluntary certification in the specific sense defined next.

Definition 12 (Voluntary Certification)   *A firm **voluntarily certifies** its product or service if it chooses to submit it to a quality rating despite not being legally required to do so.*

For example, a film production company that seeks a Motion Pictures Association film rating (PG, PG-13, etc.) for a new movie is voluntarily certifying its product. So is a college that chooses to be ranked by U.S. News & World Report. Voluntary certification is different from self-regulation because submitting to certification need not entail a significant cost. In this sense, voluntary certification may be less onerous for industry members than self-regulation as defined in Definition 11.

Voluntary certification solves a specific problem: consumer uncertainty about the attributes (quality) of the product or service they are buying. This problem is widespread. For example, parents who go to the movies with their young children may be concerned that the movie will feature explicit content. Similarly, college applicants may be uncertain about the quality of the education that they will receive at a given institution.

When, as in the above examples, consumer cannot verify a valuable feature or characteristic before purchasing the product or service, consumers may feel that the firm or the industry is not transparent. Moreover, when quality is not verifiable there is a risk that unscrupulous sellers may flood the market with subpar goods or services. These market dysfunctions inevitably create a demand for government intervention. If a credible quality certifier exists, voluntary certification can restore transparency without the need for government intervention.

Example of Voluntary Certification: Movie Ratings In the United States today, movies are rated in decreasing order of suitability for all audiences, from **G** (General audiences – All ages admitted), to **NC-17** (No one 17 and under admitted), as shown in Figure 9.2. This rating system was introduced in 1968 by the movie industry's trade association (Motion Pictures Association of America, or MPAA) when, after decades of successful self-regulation, the Hays Code had ceased being effective. By the 1960s, foreign movies were being shown in the United States that did not abide by the Code and contained very explicit content including sex and violence. Increasingly, so did domestically produced movies.

There were several reasons why movies had become more explicit in the 1960s. First, social mores had become more permissive. Second, in the so-called Miracle Decision, the Supreme Court had ruled in 1952 that film censorship was illegal.[1] And yet, despite (or, perhaps, because of) the prevalence of explicit content, the general feeling was that some populations, including children, required a wholesome fare. Thus the ratings system was created.

The goals of the ratings system were articulated by Jack Valenti, who in 1968 was the MPAA president:

> You know, I invented a ratings system, which understood two things: One, the First Amendment reigns. Freedom of speech. Freedom of content. The director is free to make any movie he wants to make and not have to cut a millimeter of it. But freedom without responsibility is anarchy. The director will know he can do that, but some of his films may be restricted from viewing by children. Now I thought that was a balancing of the moral compact.[2]

What is critical for our purpose is that the ratings system is voluntary. Movies are not required to be rated – in fact, non rated movies have their own category: **NR** (not rated). Despite this, many movies are voluntarily submitted for rating, and the ratings system works well. Fifty years after its introduction, MPAA CEO Charles H. Rivkin was able to report: "We could point to many factors behind the ratings' success. But the clearest

---

[1] The Miracle Decision concerned the censorship of a movie called *The Miracle*, which portrayed Mary's immaculate conception in a way that many felt was blasphemous.

[2] Quoted from Corliss (2007).

Voluntary certification in the movie industry.

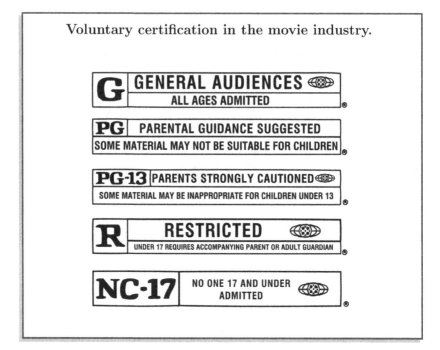

FIGURE 9.2 Motion Picture Association film rating system.

one of all comes directly from its founding mission: to maintain the trust and confidence of American parents."[3]

Example of Voluntary Certification: Automobile Safety Ratings Another example of voluntary certification is provided by the automobile safety ratings. Many car buyers value safety and will consult a car's safety ratings before purchasing it. There are two automobile ratings systems in the United States. One is administered by the National Highway Traffic Safety Administration (NHTSA, pronounced NITZ-ah). The other is administered by the Insurance Institute for Highway Safety (IIHS), a non profit financed by the insurance industry.[4] NHTSA and IIHS perform different tests and rate cars on different dimensions of crashworthiness. Both ratings are regarded as informative by consumers. As

[3] Rivkin (2018).
[4] NHTSA and IIHS do not rate all car models, only the most popular ones. New cars for sale are required to display a sticker showing the NHTSA safety score. Manufacturers are not required to disclose the IIHS scores, but the scores are published online and are very popular with car buyers.

regards whether manufacturers voluntarily submit to the rating, it is the case that many manufacturers pay for IIHS testing in circumstances where the IIHS would not test their car,[5] suggesting that manufacturers value the rating. Therefore, in this book's language, IIHS ratings are voluntary.

A noteworthy feature of automobile safety ratings is that, by definition, they rate safety features that *exceed the minimum required standards* This suggests that regulation is not the main driver of automobile safety; rather, the ratings are.[6] Indeed, automakers regularly introduce innovative safety features to ensure that their vehicles are rated favorably by NHTSA and IIHS.

Example of Voluntary Certification: College Rankings   Organizations such as US News & World Report produce widely followed rankings of US colleges and universities. These rankings are based on questionnaires that are sent to the colleges to be filled out. Most colleges fill out the questionnaires despite not being required by law to do so.

Failure to Voluntary Certify: Vehicle Emissions   The case of vehicle emissions provides an instructive contrast with safety ratings. While governments impose emission standards, to my knowledge, there are no widely-adopted private-sector ratings of car emissions.[7] This absence stands in sharp contrast to the IIHS safety ratings. This contrast suggests that, perhaps, car buyers are less interested in vehicle emissions than they are in vehicle safety and, therefore, car manufacturers have no incentive to voluntarily certify their vehicles' emissions. This point will be featured in Framework 9.

---

[5] IIHS buys most of the cars it tests, so manufacturers cannot avoid being rated: See Barry (2020). However, not all models are tested, and some manufacturers seek additional rating by the IIHS. This is the program that the IIHS calls "verification." According to the IIHS, "If a vehicle is eligible for verification, and the manufacturer wants it to receive a rating from IIHS [...] the company must conduct the test according to Institute parameters." See IIHS (2022).

[6] Federal vehicle safety standards in the US lag industry adoption and consumer demand because NHTSA is cautious about imposing new safety standards. According to Encyclopaedia Britannica, Branch (2018): "After the heady early years of the agency's existence, NHTSA regulatory programs slowed considerably, beginning in the late 1970s. Mandates for the second wave of engineering advances such as the air bag were delayed for more than a decade."

[7] At the time of this writing, a UK non profit called Allow Independent Road-testing (AIR) is attempting to set up a non governmental rating system for vehicle emissions. This enterprise is admirable, but, so far, the rating system has not been widely adopted.

Why Enforcement Is Not Required   What is the force that drives firms to voluntarily certify the quality of their product or service, even when that quality is not so good? To rephrase the question more concretely, take a movie that has some explicit content, such that its rating is foreseeably, say, an **R** (under 17 must be accompanied by a parent). Why would the movie producers submit this movie for rating? Or, why would a college that anticipates being ranked as middling, fill out the US News and World Report questionnaire?

The answer lies in a branch of economic theory called voluntary certification theory.[8] This theory predicts that, if credible certification is freely available to firms, all firms will submit to it, even the ones that expect not to fare well. Here is the logic. Posit a situation where no firm submits to certification – and watch it unravel. The unraveling starts from the firm with the highest quality q_1 (in the case of movies, that would be a Disney movie; in the case of colleges, that may be Harvard). It is perfectly rational for this firm to voluntarily submit to certification because its quality is the highest. So the best firm will voluntarily certify and, thus, separate itself from the average firm. Now, take the firm with the second-highest quality q_2. If this firm does not certify its quality, consumers will not be able to distinguish it from all other uncertified firms. Since this firm has the best quality among all the uncertified firms, it is better off disclosing its quality. So the second-best firm will also voluntarily submit to certification. Now take the firm with the third-highest quality q_3, and repeat the process until *all* firms, including those of middling and even low quality, except possibly the absolutely worst firm, find it expedient to certify their quality.

This argument proves something that is quite intuitive: In the presence of a credible quality certifier, firms should be willing to submit themselves to certification even if their quality is not good. The logic is that they can't afford not to, lest they be lumped with the worst of the worst. In economic theory, this logic is called "information unraveling."

Theorem 2 (Unraveling Theorem)   *The mere presence of a credible quality certifier leads firms to submit themselves to certification even if their quality is not good.*

Industry Fundamentals That Promote Voluntary Certification   The unraveling logic that leads firms to voluntarily submit to certification is quite

---

[8]   This literature originated with Grossman (1981).

powerful. Still, there are some basic requirement for the unraveling to work.

First, there must be a hidden quality problem: Consumers must not be able to verify the quality themselves, else firms would not need to be certified. Second, there must be a credible certifier that consumers trust, else firms would not benefit from certification. Third, consumers must be willing to pay more for higher quality; else higher-quality firms don't benefit from certification and the unraveling logic fails. Fourth, there must be a "best firm" with the highest quality, to get the unraveling process started.

Framework 9: Industry fundamentals that promote voluntary certification

1. Quality is hidden from consumers
2. There is a credible certifier
3. Consumers are willing to pay for quality
4. Some products have higher quality than others.

Applying Framework 9 to the Movie Industry after 1952 In the movie industry after the 1952 Miracle Decision, all the items in Framework 9 check out. First, quality was hidden from consumers prior to the act of consumption: Parents didn't know how much explicit content a movie would have until they went to the theater and watched the movie. Second, a credible certifier existed: It was the Classification and Ratings Administration (CARA), which was set up by the MPAA as an independent division. CARA was a group of individuals called *raters* who watched any movie that was voluntarily submitted to CARA, rated it using the system in Figure 9.2, and then released the rating publicly.[9] CARA's credibility as a certifier has been established over fifty years of rating movies. Third, consumers (parents, in this case) were willing to pay to watch a movie with their family, but only if the movie was known not to contain explicit material. Therefore, demand was higher for those movies. (In this case, high quality corresponds to less explicit content.) Fourth, some movies had less explicit content, that is, they were of higher quality than others. In sum, all the fundamentals were in place for voluntary certification to emerge in the movie industry post-1952.

---

[9] Movies can be submitted for rating at www.carafilmratings.com/, and the public can search for a movie's rating at www.filmratings.com/.

Applying Framework 9 to the Higher Education Industry All the items in Framework 9 were in place for voluntary certification to emerge in the higher education industry. The quality of a college's educational product was difficult to know for most parents and students. US News & World Report's credibility rested on the fact that it had no conflict of interest with the colleges. Parents and students were willing to pay for a good education. Finally, some colleges provided better education than others. Therefore, we expect voluntary certification to emerge in higher education. Interestingly, in the case of colleges, the certifier is a for-profit, meaning that US News & World Report actually makes money by providing a certification service.

Applying Framework 9 to Emission Ratings All the fundamentals in Framework 9 are in place for vehicle emissions, except for one: At the time of this writing, consumer demand for low emissions was not so strong that car manufacturers were incentivized to voluntarily certify their vehicles above and beyond the certification process required by law. Therefore, voluntary certification failed to emerge for vehicle emissions.

Learning Points Voluntary certification solves a specific problem: consumer uncertainty about the attributes (quality) of the product or service they are buying. Submitting to voluntary certification is neither mandatory, nor necessarily costly for firms. In this sense, voluntary certification is less onerous for industry members than self-regulation. Under the conditions spelled out in Framework 9, the mere presence of a quality certifier leads firms to submit themselves to certification – even firms whose quality is not good.

9.3 TAKEAWAYS FROM THIS CHAPTER

Industries often find themselves at risk of clumsy government regulation. There are two common triggers of government intervention. The first is that the regulators don't like the industry's product or service. The second is that consumers cannot verify product quality and the market is potentially awash with inferior products. It is in the industry's best interest to preemptively address these problems and remove the triggers of government intervention.

If the problem is that regulators don't like the industry's product or service, self-regulation is the answer. The sector should create a suitable code of conduct and enforce it against deviating firms. Successfully enforcing self-regulation requires the particular set of market fundamentals listed in Framework 8 at page 119. If these fundamentals are not in place, self-regulation will fail because it cannot be self-enforced. When the problem is that the customer cannot verify quality and the market is awash with inferior products, voluntary certification is the answer. The industry should set up a credible certifier. Voluntary certification does not require the market fundamentals listed in the box at page 119, but it requires that the conditions listed in Framework 9 at page 129 hold. A trade association can be helpful in coordinating either strategy.

10

Windows of Opportunity

Because the rules of the competitive game are tremendously flexible, there are few limits to the amount of change that can be achieved through SBM. For example, at the time of this writing the top marginal income tax rate was 37 percent, but it has been as high as 94 percent (in 1944) and as low as zero (before 1913).[1] Similarly, the production and sales of alcoholic beverages, flourishing today, was entirely prohibited between 1920 and 1933. Union rules have changed over time, too, with more US states adopting "right to work" laws that make it more difficult for unions to organize. All these are major changes in the rules of the competitive game. Therefore, it may seem that, in SBM, "all options are on the table at any time." This is not quite the case.

In practice, there are limits to what can be achieved by SBM at any given moment. Ideas that are too far from the status quo cannot even be entertained, so the practical options are limited to a window around the status quo. This is called the Overton window. Recognizing the existence of the Overton window, and what it takes to shift it, is the subject of Section 10.1. Moreover, legislative (as opposed to regulatory) change does not happen gradually over time. Instead, change is punctuated: The status quo lasts for a long time and then, suddenly, all the change happens at once. Therefore, when SBM involves a legislative change, there are narrow windows of opportunity. This is the subject of Section 10.2.

10.1 OVERTON WINDOW

Definition of Overton Window   The Overton window is named after Joseph Overton, a Michigan engineer who, in his second career, became a

---

[1] York (2021), Wolters Kluwer (2013).

policy activist. Overton devised a concept he originally named "window of discourse" (the name was later changed in his honor) to describe how policy change takes place in democracies. Here is a description.

The simplest definition ... is the Overton window describes a range of public policy options. The options inside that window are safe for elected officials to support without getting unelected and the ones outside the window are not yet safe for public officials to support, because they'll risk getting unelected. So our job in the think tank world, in the journalism world, and in in the religious world, and in the education world – our job is to change what is acceptable by society because the politicians will eventually follow.[2]

There are three main insights in this description of the Overton window. First, not all changes that are technologically feasible are politically viable: Some are just too extreme – in either direction: See Figure 10.1. Second, the window evolves over time: What is unacceptable today may be acceptable tomorrow, and vice versa. Third, the evolution of the window is driven by society, not by politicians. Next is my definition of the Overton window.

Definition 13 (Overton Window) *The Overton window is the set of policy options that are fit to discuss and entertain seriously at any given time.*

Note that this definition does not require the window to be the same for society as a whole. Different societal groups may have different Overton windows, that is, different views about whether a policy is radical or not. It is possible, for example, for a given policy to be seen as acceptable by physicians or psychologists, but as radical by the rest of society, as will be the case in the discussion at pages 134 and ff.

Figure 10.1 illustrates the Overton window in an abstract context. Normally, the Overton window includes the current policy and, in addition, some "nearby" policies that are perceived by the public to be close enough to the status quo to be considered sensible or at least acceptable. Some policies, however, are too far from the status quo. These are labeled "radical," or even "unthinkable."

The Overton Window in the Pink Viagra Case The following example illustrates the Overton window using the Pink Viagra case in Section 2.7.

---

[2] This definition is transcribed from an interview by Joseph Lehman, the president of the think tank that created the term Overton window. See Acton Institute (2022) at min 24:40 and ff.

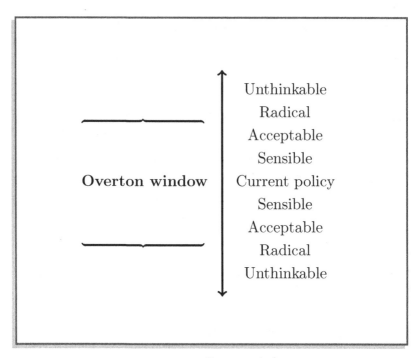

FIGURE 10.1 Overton window.

At the top of the vertical scale in Figure 10.2, I listed attitudes toward female sexuality that I believe were commonly held 100 years ago; at the bottom, attitudes I believe are commonly held today. The figure is impressionistic: It is not based on survey data, and my goal is not to accurately describe attitudes a hundred years ago, or even today. Rather, the figure is intended to illustrate two points. First, not everything that is technically possible is politically feasible: Much of the lower half of the vertical scale in Figure 10.2 was technically possible a hundred years ago, but no politician could have advocated for such policies and be reelected. Hence, these policies are located outside the 1910 Overton window. Second, what most people in 1910 would consider unthinkable (women boosting their sexual desire with pharmaceuticals, totally outside the 1910 Overton window) is today's clever business idea. Conversely, what is unthinkable today (repression of female sexual desire, well outside today's Overton window) would, I imagine, be considered less unthinkable, or even acceptable, many years ago.

What It Takes to Shift the Overton Window   The Pink Viagra case provides a good illustration of some of the forces that move the Overton

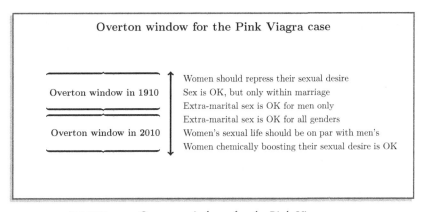

FIGURE 10.2 Overton windows for the Pink Viagra case.

window. I have described the multipronged push at page 111. I review it here and provide additional color:

1. Even before Addyi was invented, the pharmaceutical industry had long engaged in "disease branding" through the funding of continuing education for physicians. According to Meixel et al. (2014): "Hypoactive sexual desire disorder was established by industry in 2004 to prepare the market for a testosterone patch for women."

    Part of this effort included "free, internet-based, industry funded, accredited CME modules."[3] Sprout Pharmaceutical's campaign benefited from these preparatory steps.

2. Sprout's campaign hired as an advocate a former director of the FDA's Office of Women's Health. She proceeded to recruit women's organizations into the "26-0" coalition. In a meeting with feminist health leaders, the former regulator advocated for Addyi by raising the sexism issue.[4]

3. Sprout's campaign created a coalition of twenty-six women's rights and women's health organizations, including the National Organization for Women (NOW). In a press release the day after Addyi was approved by the FDA, NOW stated: "Women – no less than men – deserve to have satisfactory sexual experiences and fulfilling intimate relationships."[5]

[3] Meixel et al. (2014).
[4] Block and Canner (2016).
[5] National Organization for Women (2015).

4. Eleven members of Congress wrote to the FDA, stating:

> We firmly believe that equitable access to health care should be a funda-
> mental right, regardless of whether you are a man or a woman. But when
> it comes to sexual health – and, in particular, sexual dysfunction – that is
> not the case. Today in America there are 26 FDA approved drugs marketed
> for male sexual dysfunction and not a single treatment yet approved for the
> most common form of female sexual dysfunction.

5. More than 60,000 people signed a change.org petition to the FDA,
   stating: "Do you believe that women deserve equal treatment when
   it comes to sex? ... Help us tell the FDA it is time to make #HER-
   Story and approve the first-ever HSDD medical treatment option
   for women!"[6]

Step 1 indicates that the pharmaceutical industry was moving the Overton window *for some physicians* even before the Sprout campaign had
been conceived. With step 1, the pharmaceutical industry had established
among some physicians and health care professionals that insufficient sexual desire could be a disease. The result was to bring low sexual desire
into the realm of professional conversation. This effort took many years,
but it successfully moved the Overton window *for some physicians.* As a
result, increasing low sexual desire could be discussed as a legitimate professional goal instead of being dismissed as absurd. This was the starting
point from which Sprout Pharmaceuticals' campaign was developed.

The ultimate target of Sprout's campaign were current FDA regulators.
An enlarged Overton window among physicians was necessary, but not
sufficient to get regulators to approve Addyi. Indeed, the regulators dealt
with the data in the application, not with theoretical societal issues. They
followed a well-defined process which entailed trading off a drug's safety
with its effectiveness. In the regulators' minds, the trade-off was not to
Addyi's advantage, as witnessed by two consecutive denials.

So, the next step was to increase the cost to the regulators of denying
the application. This was done by threatening the regulators' reputation
for competence in the court of public opinion (steps 2–5). To reach public
opinion, the issue would have to be covered extensively by the media. A
moral narrative was required for the media to cover the story. A moral
narrative comprises three elements: a hero, a villain, and a victim. In the
media's narrative, the role of victim would be played by women who suffered from insufficient sexual desire; the role of hero would be played

---

[6] www.change.org/p/womendeserve-equal-treatment-when-it-comes-to-sex

by the drug; and the role of villain would be played by the FDA regulators. Casting FDA scientists in a negative light could be difficult: Their expertise was not a viable target of attack because the FDA enjoyed a strong reputation for expertise. So, it was necessary to cast doubt on their motives. This was done by introducing gender bias: Couching the media narrative in this framing would be credible with society at large. It is worth noting that the message in steps 2–5 was coordinated and focused on bias. In my view, this coordination was a deliberate strategy to threaten the regulators' reputation for competence in the court of public opinion.

The combined effect of the shift of the Overton window *for some physicians*, and of a media narrative that cast FDA regulators as potential villains, was to shift the public's perception from "insufficient sexual desire is not a disease," to "some physicians say that insufficient sexual desire is a disease, many women seem to suffer from it, and it would not necessarily be wrong to pressure the (possibly biased) FDA regulators to approve the drug."

The shift in the Overton window for physicians, and the media's public indictment of the regulators' motives, put pressure on the regulators. Even if they personally felt doubtful about Addyi, regulators are human: They interact with their professional peers, with their families, and with the rest of society. Nobody likes to be accused of being biased, even if the accusations are uninformed. Moreover, the FDA's reputation with the public could be hurt. With their reputation under attack, the regulators gave in and approved the drug.

The general lesson from the Pink Viagra case is that to change the regulators' mind about the drug, it took a change in the Overton window among physicians first ("disease branding,") then an attack on the regulators' motives in the court of public opinion. The media played a huge role in the latter, but not in the former. In my judgment, politics played a minor role: The big lift was done by professional and societal peer pressure.

The Pink Viagra case suggests that the Overton window is shifted mostly by professional and societal peer effects, not primarily by politicians.

Who Controls the Overton Window I make the assumption that the boundaries of public discourse can be changed by trusted sources (scientists, or members in one's professional community) and by the people among whom the discourse takes place (one's friendship network). If this assumption is correct, then Figure 10.3 provides a useful ranking of the most influential shifters of the Overton window.

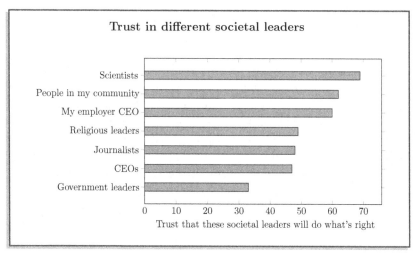

FIGURE 10.3 Legislators less trusted to "do what's right" than media and experts. Average from a 9-point scale. Respondents drawn from US general population. Source: 2021 Edelman Trust Barometer.

Figure 10.3 indicates that the most trusted societal leaders are scientists, people in one's local community, and own employers. Scientists are at the top. Regulators may be thought of as scientists. Activists may be thought of as a combination of "Scientists" and "People in my local community." When scientists, regulators, activists, and the media coalesce on a narrative, people in the community change their views and the Overton window shifts.

Elected officials don't generally control the narrative because they are not trusted by the public: Figure 10.3 indicates that, in the United States, "government leaders" are the least trusted among societal leaders. Public trust in government has trended down over a sixty-year span, recently reaching historic lows. In 2022, only one-fifth of Americans said they could trust the government in Washington to do what is right "just about always" or "most of the time."[7] With elected officials being less trusted now than ever before, their ability to shape public discourse is at its lowest. This is not a hard-and-fast rule, of course. Some elected officials occasionally do shift the Overton window, but this rarely happens against the consensus of scientists, activists, regulators, and the media. Most of

---

[7] See Pew Research Center (2022) for the evolution of trust in government since the 1960s.

the time elected officials react to, rather than drive shifts in the Overton window.

In sum, media, activists, and regulators are better placed than legislators to shape public discourse.

Effect of the Overton Windows on Elected Officials The Overton window is constantly pushed and pulled by the media, by activists, and by regulators. Elected officials, on their part, know that they will be held accountable in the next election, not today (refer back to Section 4.2), at which time the Overton window may have shifted. Even if a policy if popular today, unforeseen shifts in the Overton window may prevent elected officials from claiming credit in the future. This makes elected officials cautious to move on issues where the Overton window is fluid. These are precisely the policies where the media, activists, and regulators are active.

Consider, for example, the policy of constraining fossil fuel production to slow down climate change. If production is made more difficult, the price of fossil fuels is bound to increase in the short run. Such increases are intuitively unpopular with voters: Voters are liable to vote out elected officials when fuel prices are high. However, voters are also swayed – to some degree – by the consensus among regulators, scientists, media, and activists that climate change is very dangerous.[8] As long as that "danger narrative" is expected to grow in the voters' minds (the media play a large role here), a forward-looking elected official will be cautious about supporting fossil fuel production, even if there is a large coalition in favor of low fuel prices now, because it will be difficult to claim credit for these actions in the next election.

This example illustrates that even if a large coalition is currently supportive of a policy (e.g., motorists in favor of lower fuel prices), this may not be enough to gain an elected official's support: When election time comes around, the legislator will need a favorable, or at least a not-unfavorable, narrative in support of his/her actions, and s/he may not get it if the views of regulators, activists, and media converge against it.

A good indicator that the Overton window is stable and unlikely to shift in the future, is that Interests with opposing political orientations converge on the same narrative. This was the case, for example, when activist groups from both the left and the right opposed the 2008 bailout

---

[8] I am assuming here that regulators, scientists, and activist have reached a consensus that climate change is very dangerous.

of the financial industry (refer to Section 2.1). The Overton window has not shifted to this day: The bailout of the financial industry is still seen as, a necessary evil at best, despite our present knowledge that the bailouts actually ended up making a lot of money for the government (see footnote 1 at page 51).

Learning Points   The Overton window is the set of policy options that a politician can support without losing the next election. Outside the Overton window lies the radical, the unsayable, and the unthinkable. The Overton window moves all the time under the action of, among others, the media, activists, and regulators. It is possible for industry to move the Overton window, as the pharmaceutical industry did in the Pink Viagra case. While most elected officials rarely move the Overton window, all elected officials are very attuned to its evolution.

10.2 POLICY WINDOWS

Changes in legislation are like earthquakes: They happen not at all, and then all at once. Are there indicators or warning signs that a change in law is becoming possible – or even likely? In the student debt relief case of Section 2.4, for example, could the big banks have detected some warning signs, and exited the student loan market before it was too late? If such warning signs could be identified in general, beyond the specifics of a given industry, that would be helpful to the SBM practitioner.

Motivated by the observation that laws (as opposed to regulations) change rarely but bigly, John Kingdon, a political scientist at the University of Michigan, set out to answer a critical question: What circumstances must occur in order for a law to change? Or, put differently: Among the many issues and problems that affect our society, which ones make it to the top of the heap and are addressed legislatively?

To answer this question, Kingdon interviewed government officials, congressional staff, and interest groups, about the process through which laws change. He was interested in how problems become recognized, policies emerge, are processed by the political system, and finally result in new legislation. Kingdon found that legislative change happens when three so-called streams converge: the streams of *problems*, *policies*, and *politics*. Henceforth, I will capitalize these terms when it is worth emphasizing that I am using them in the technical sense defined below.

Problems, Policies, and Politics   The streams of Problems and Policies are defined as follows: "[Problems are] concerns that individuals inside and outside the policy system have. Policies (solutions) are people's products, usually generated in narrow policy communities; they are answers that may be produced not only when needed."[9]

By noting that Policies are produced "not only when needed," the quote draws attention to the class of professional policy experts, analysts, pundits, academics, NGO members, and so on that are continually coming up with solutions to problems that they think are important. The stream of Politics is defined as follows: "The politics stream consists of three elements: the national mood, pressure group campaigns, and administrative or legislative turnover."[10]

Problems, Policies, and Politics in the Student Debt Relief Case of Section 2.4   In the student debt context of Section 2.4, the Problem was that, by circa 2020, 30 percent of US adults had incurred some student debt, with the median debtor owing more than $20,000. This was a Problem for a wide set of stakeholders: first, American individuals and families. Second, the financial institutions holding the debt. Third, potentially, for the financial sector as a whole which might be destabilized if the debt was summarily canceled.

The Policies were the proposed solutions to the problem of student debt. These included: lowering interest rates and forgiving debt for current debtors; guardrails against future debt accumulation; rationalizing the existing debt relief programs; expanding federal grants for education; and making college tuition free.[11] The "narrow policy community" that generated these policy solutions included academics in the fields of education, psychology, law, and economics. Beyond that, nonprofit organizations such as the Student Debt Crisis Center, think tanks such as the Brookings Institution,[12] financial and education regulators.[13]

The Politics included which party was in power (the US Democratic Party was more aligned with debtors, students, and young people), how the nation felt about debt cancellation/forgiveness, and the presence of a strong activist network in favor of debt relief.

Problems, policies, and politics are referred to as *streams* in order to evoke the idea that they are constantly bubbling and they normally flow in

---

[9] Zahariadis (2019), p. 69.
[10] Zahariadis (2019), p. 73.
[11] See Helhoski (2021).
[12] Looney et al. (2020).
[13] Searching for "student debt crisis" on Google and Google Scholar uncovers a good portion of the policy community.

separate channels. Thus, the problem stream is filled with the social problems that, in any given moment, are seen as pressing by the public or a subset thereof. The policy stream "is filled with the output of experts and analysts who examine problems and propose solutions. In this stream, the myriad possibilities for policy action and inaction are identified, assessed, and narrowed down to a subset of ostensibly feasible options."[14]

Policy Windows   We now come to the key concept. According to Kingdon: "The separate streams of problems, policies, and politics come together at certain critical times. Solutions become joined to problems, and both of them are joined to favorable political forces."[15]

When the three streams are momentarily joined, a policy window opens up. "The combination of all three streams into a single package dramatically enhances the chances that a specific policy will be adopted by policy makers."[16] According to Kingdon:

windows are opened either by the appearance of compelling problems or by happenings in the political stream. . . . Policy entrepreneurs, people who are willing to invest their resources in pushing their pet proposals or problems, are responsible not only for prompting important people to pay attention, but also for coupling solutions to problems and for coupling both problems and solutions to politics.[17]

Definition 14 (Policy Window)   *A policy window is the moment in time in which a policy entrepreneur manages to bring together the streams of problems, policies, and politics.*

A policy entrepreneur, in Kingdon's theory, is someone – a politician, a lobbyist, or an activist – who can bring these streams together. In the student debt case of Section 2.4, the Chairwoman of the House Financial Services Committee was acting as a policy entrepreneur.

What Are the Signs of a Window Opening?   It is by definition difficult to predict when a policy window will open. For example, in the student loans case, JP Morgan Chase had started tapering down the issuance of new student loans in 2012, and in September 2013 it stopped issuing new student loans entirely. In 2017, furthermore, it completely divested and sold its entire education loans portfolio, worth $6.9 billion, to Navient.[18]

---

[14] Beland and Howlett (2016).
[15] Kingdon (1984), p. 21.
[16] Zahariadis (2019), p. 65.
[17] Kingdon (1984), p. 21.
[18] Kirkham (2020). In 2019 Navient was sued by thirty-nine US states for predatory lending, and ended up settling for $1.85 billion.

What predictors did Chase's CEO see, that led him to divest Chase from student debt? Let's apply Kingdon's three-streams paradigm.

Chase's Problem Stream around 2012 Around 2012, the student debt problem was getting larger. By then, one in four families spent more than 11 percent of their take-home income on student loans, or more than $300 out of a $3,000 family income.[19] At any given time, of those borrowers who had started repaying their loans, only 41 percent were current.[20] Moreover, low-income families were less likely to make consistent loan payments (44 percent) than high-income families (63 percent).

Chase's Policies Stream around 2012 A number of academics, regulators, and pundits were offering clever fixes for the student debt problem. But, more importantly, some tried-and-true solutions were available: Back in 2007, President G. W. Bush had introduced the principle of "income-based repayment" for federal student loans. In 2007, loan payments were capped at 15 percent of the borrower's income and the loan would be forgiven after 25 years of payment. The policy was controversial when it was adopted, and other provisions of the law caused some private lenders to exit the student loan market. But, overall, the policy ended up working as intended.

The importance of having tried-and-true solutions cannot be overestimated. Politicians are very concerned about unintended consequences, and with good reason: Refer back to the discussion of legislators' status quo bias in Section 4.2. So policies that have been tried before, and have worked well, are especially focal. In 2011, President Obama proposed a tweak on President Bush's tried-and-true solution: The cap on loan payments would be lowered to 10 percent of the borrower's income, and the forgiveness date would be lowered to twenty years.

Let's tell another one million students that when they graduate, they will be required to pay only 10 percent of their income on student loans, and all of their debt will be forgiven after 20 years — and forgiven after 10 years if they choose a career in public service, because in the United States of America, no one should go broke because they chose to go to college.[21]

President Obama's tweak had not yet become law in 2012.

Chase's Politics Stream around 2012 The media frequently used the term "student debt crisis" or "college debt crisis" in reference to the

---

[19] Farrell et al. (2019), page 6, finding 1.
[20] Farrell et al. (2019), Table 1.2.
[21] The White House (2011).

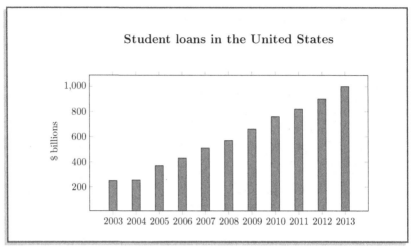

FIGURE 10.4 Student loan debt in the United States. Reproduced from Severns (2013).

student debt problem. In a 2013 article titled "The Student Loan Debt Crisis in 9 Charts," the left-of-center periodical *Mother Jones* published a graphic showing the steady growth of student debt (Figure 10.4). The chart showed that outstanding student debt had quadrupled in the decade 2003–13, and had passed the symbolic $1 trillion threshold in 2012.[22] This dramatic coverage, and President Obama's advocacy, were tugging on the Overton window for student debt: It was now accepted that the federal government was to some extent responsible for the plight of student debtors.

In 2012, student debt became a campaign issue, leading to a spike in media focus.[23] Two-thirds of voters under the age of thirty had student loans. The fact that President Obama seemed likely to be reelected meant that he could use the power of the presidential office to continue pushing for student debt relief.

Chases's Exit Decision In 2012 the three streams of problem, policy, and politics seemed poised to come together. At the very least, they were too close for Chase's comfort. First, the social problem was undoubtedly significant, and it was not going to go away. Second, a tried-and-true policy solution existed which could be further tweaked incrementally to further relieve debtors. Finally, a good portion of the country had become

---

[22] Gitlen (2022).
[23] See Leetaru (2021).

accustomed to the idea that the government would look after student debtors. The accumulation of these considerations made it likely that the government would take some action on student debt. Therefore, it was wise for Chase (and the other big banks, too) to divest from the market.

Learning Points Laws (as opposed to regulations) change rarely, but, when they do, they change significantly. What factors predict a legislative change? According to the policy windows model, three streams must be brought together: problems, policies, and politics. When these streams are brought together by a policy entrepreneur, a policy window opens. Then, there is a chance that new legislation might pass.

10.3 TAKEAWAYS FROM THIS CHAPTER

Business leaders should pay attention to shifts in the Overton window that threaten to make their business model Radical or even Unthinkable. These shifts generally happen slowly: In the student loan industry, it took years for the Overton window to move. However, the Overton window can shift quickly during crises. Activist groups and policy think tanks are continually at work shifting the Overton window. Chapter 6 provides some strategies for business to tug at the Overton window.

The Overton window is part of a larger model, Kingdon's policy windows paradigm. This paradigm predicts that shifts in legislation happen when three elements (or streams) come together: problem, policy, and politics. Business should be aware of these streams and act preemptively, as the big banks did by exiting the student loan market around 2012.

I I

SBM in Society

I have come to the conclusion that politics are too serious a matter to be left to the politicians.

Charles de Gaulle

As I often tried to remind people, no one elected us. . . . As a general principle, it seemed more sensible to ask an elected government to regulate companies than to ask unelected companies to regulate such a government.

Brad Smith
President of Microsoft[1]

Americans hold a dim view of business advocacy. According to a 2018 survey, 53 percent of Americans viewed the role of lobbyists and special interests in Washington as "a big problem."[2] Worse, in a 2020 survey of the honesty of professions, lobbyists ranked dead last – below car salesmen.[3] This dim view of business advocacy is, in my opinion, largely unwarranted. Still, it makes sense to ask whether society would be better off by limiting SBM, or by changing the way that it is done. In this chapter I address two related questions: Would it be desirable to restrict the business sector's ability to advocate? And, should corporations be encouraged to interface with society in a different way?

In Section 11.1, I make the case that, if business was restricted in its ability to communicate with government officials, the officials would

---

[1] Smith and Browne (2021), p. 251.
[2] By comparison, in the same survey, only 38 percent viewed illegal immigration as "a big problem": see Bombardini and Trebbi (2020).
[3] Saad (2022).

likely make decisions less accurately, but not any more independently of business. In Section 11.2, furthermore, I argue that allowing relatively unfettered business advocacy can help ensure that regulations are innovation-friendly and, moreover, that in comparison to other political systems, the US openness to business advocacy actually promotes innovation. These two sections, when taken together, amount to a cautious case against restricting business advocacy.

In Section 11.3, I move away from business advocacy as characterized in Definition 2 to discuss a different way in which business organizations operate in the political arena: namely, the leveraging of the business organization's relationship with its customers, suppliers, or workers to pursue societal goals not directly tied to its own business. I argue that this behavior, despite being well intentioned and popular with a segment of public opinion, should be approached with some caution by business corporations.

11.1 AN INFORMATION-SPECIFIC CASE AGAINST RESTRICTING BUSINESS ADVOCACY

A large part of business advocacy, as characterized in Definition 2, amounts essentially to communicating soft information to government officials.[4] In this section I outline a logical case for permitting unlimited communication of soft information between business and government officials. The argument is based on the economic theory of cheap talk.[5]

According to this theory, a sender who has private soft information (a lobbyist, he) can, by communicating it to a receiver (a government official, she), improve the receiver's ability to take appropriate action (regulate in an informed manner). The sender will communicate only to the extent that he benefits from the communication. To the degree that sender and receiver do not perfectly agree on the ideal regulation, the sender will strategically obfuscate and communicate less than transparently. However, the degree of obfuscation will not make the receiver's action any more skewed toward the sender's ideal action. In other words, the sender's bias does not propagate to the receiver's decision rule – regardless of how much information is transmitted. If the sender is forbidden from communicating, therefore, the receiver's decisions will become less accurate, but no better aligned with her own ideal point.

---

4 For a definition of soft information, refer to Definition 10 at page 101.
5 Crawford and Sobel (1982).

This theory predicts that the sender is unable to systematically skew the receiver's decision rule *despite having monopoly power over the information*. When the sender lacks such monopoly power, such as when there are two senders, the theory is even more optimistic: It predicts that the receiver will be able to extract so much information from the two senders, that she will be able to implement her preferred full-information decision.[6] In other words, enlarging the set of agents who are allowed to communicate improves the receiver's ability to accurately pursue her own goals – again, without systematically skewing her decisions toward the senders' ideal points. The above discussion is summarized in the following theorem.

Theorem 3 (Fundamental Theorem of Information Transmission) *If the set of senders who are allowed to transmit soft information to a receiver is restricted, either from two to one or from one to zero, the receiver's decisions will become less accurate but no more aligned with her own preferences. Therefore, information transmission must be facilitated, not restricted.*

When applied to the real world, this theory suggests that restricting the ability of business to communicate with government officials cannot affect the officials' goals. The only effect that restricting communication can have is to decrease the accuracy of the officials' decisions. At the root of this theoretical prediction is the fact that, whether or not communication is restricted, the government official retains the ultimate decision power; therefore, the official will utilize whatever information she is able to obtain in the single-minded pursuit of her own goals.

Learning Points   Economic theory suggests that restricting the ability of business to communicate with government officials will not make the officials' decision-making any more independent of the goals of business, but it will reduce the accuracy of the officials' decisions.

11.2 AN INNOVATION-BASED CASE AGAINST RESTRICTING
BUSINESS ADVOCACY

The previous section has argued against restricting the ability of business to communicate with government. The argument was grounded in an economic theory that rests on a foundational assumption: that sender and receiver cannot write explicit or implicit contracts restricting

---

[6] Battaglini (2002).

the receiver's freedom of action. In reality, this assumption may be violated. For example, the notion of business advocacy as a legislative subsidy, which is discussed at page 47, could be interpreted as an implicit contract – a quid pro quo – between advocates and legislators. In this case, we are outside the scope of the theory featured in Section 11.1 and, in principle, restricting the ability of some or all firms to implicitly contract with government officials, that is, to engage in business advocacy, might be prosocial.

In this section, I argue that, as a practical matter, any restrictions placed on business advocacy are likely to constrain younger and smaller firms more so than large and established ones. The former, more than the latter, are likely to advocate for innovation-friendly regulatory changes. Therefore, with more rules against business advocacy, pro-innovation advocacy is disfavored relative to pro-status quo advocacy.[7] The argument proceeds in steps.

For Innovation to Be Deployed, Regulations Must Change Often, regulations must change for innovation to be deployed. For example, Uber's "gig driving" business model ran afoul of legacy taxi regulations that required drivers-for-hire to own a taxi license. In many cities, licenses were limited in number and owned by incumbents. Complying with existing regulations would have required Uber drivers, or Uber itself, to purchase taxi licenses, which would have been prohibitively expensive for Uber. This example illustrates why the deployment of innovation requires regulations to evolve – in this case, permitting non licensed drivers to be hired by paying passengers.

Business Advocacy Is Necessary to Change Regulation In theory, regulations could evolve from the top down, that is, without any impulse from the business sector. In practice, however, business advocacy is a prime mover of regulatory evolution. Uber, for example, had to fight mightily in many jurisdictions to secure a license to operate. It is doubtful that the regulatory changes that Uber needed could or would have been initiated from the top down, that is, by local governments, without Uber's disruptive advocacy. This example illustrates that an innovative challenger had to engage in business advocacy (fighting the local taxi industry in each jurisdiction) in order to make regulation evolve and, in this way, earn a license to operate.

---

[7] Due to the broad nature of the question, in this section I do not distinguish between advocacy with elected officials and regulators, but, rather, I talk about rule makers.

It make sense that regulatory evolution should be driven by the private sector rather than by the government. First, innovative businesses know about cutting-edge technologies: The government, in contrast, knows little about presently available technologies, and even less about future ones. Uber, for example, knew of a new way to transport people from point A to point B. At an abstract level, this was knowledge about a future technology that the government did not have and was not equipped to evaluate. But the business sector, and in particular venture capitalists, could evaluate Uber's new technology. They liked it, and their seal of approval manifested itself in copious investment. This shows that the private sector understood that Uber's technology was innovative but the government did not.

Second, anyone seeking to change the rules of the competitive game must invest a lot of time and effort. Often, only the businesses that benefit financially from changing the rules of the game have the incentive to invest the required time and effort. For example, when Uber undertook its bruising regulatory and legislative fights with local governments, it was motivated by a considerable financial reward.

However, Business Advocacy Can Also Stifle Innovation Incumbent firms often use business advocacy to prevent entry and to stifle innovative competitors. For example, the legacy taxi industry sought to use existing regulations (taxi licenses) to stop Uber's technology from being deployed. While the taxi industry was unsuccessful in the United States, it succeeded in Europe: in many European countries, the taxi industry was able to hamstring Uber's operations. This is a case where business advocacy was successfully deployed by incumbents to stifle innovation.

When Is Business Advocacy More Likely to Promote Innovation, than to Stifle It? SBM often pits unimaginative incumbents against innovative challengers. Typically, incumbents have an advantage in SBM because they have better connections and more-established trust relationships with government officials, than challengers do. This incumbency advantage may result in the stifling of innovation.

Intuitively, if incumbents enjoy preferential access to the political system and are able to act as gatekeepers for younger and more dynamic firms, it is more likely that incumbents will succeed in protecting the status quo, and innovative entrants may not get the chance to advocate for a change in the rules of the game. If, instead, innovative firms enjoy somewhat comparable access to the political system as established firms do, then all firms can advocate on an equal footing and, presumably, the firm advocating for the best regulation will win because, ultimately, its technology creates more value.

This argument suggests that political systems that are more open to business advocacy should give rise to more innovation-friendly regulations. The logic is that when access to the political system is limited, it is more likely to be controlled by corporate incumbents. Put differently, when advocacy is made more difficult, the "marginal firm" that is shut out of the advocacy game is more likely to be a new and innovative one, than an established incumbent.

Hypothesis: Open Access Promotes Innovation The above discussion suggests a hypothesis: innovation-friendly regulations should be more likely to emerge in political systems where access to the political arena is relatively available to all firms. Conversely, in political systems where the incumbents control access to the political arena, they may be able to block the adoption of innovation-friendly regulations.

This hypothesis can be tested, at least informally, because political systems vary in the degree to which they are open to business advocacy. As described in Section 3.4, in pluralistic systems like the United States, the political system is more open to business advocacy by all manner of businesses, than in corporatist systems like those in European countries, where access to the political system is limited and controlled by corporate incumbents.[8] The above discussion suggest that pluralistic political systems, being more open to corporate advocacy, should give rise to more pro-innovation regulations than corporatist political systems, where access is funneled through hierarchical trade associations that are controlled by market incumbents.

Hypothesis 1 *Pluralistic political systems, being more open to business advocacy, should give rise to more pro-innovation regulations, than corporatist political systems where access to the political system is limited and controlled by market incumbents. Nondemocratic political systems, which are the least open to business advocacy, should give rise to the least-innovation friendly regulations.*

The fact that Uber was able to change the rules of the competitive game in the United States (pluralist) but not in Europe (corporatist) conforms with this hypothesis. But this is just an example. Whether Hypothesis 1 is true in general is an empirical question.

---

[8] Refer to the comparison of corporatism and pluralism in Section 3.4.

TABLE 11.1 *Largest US and EU companies, by capitalization on September 1, 2021.*

Largest US companies are newer and more innovative than EU ones			
US Companies	Founded	EU Companies	Founded
Apple	1976	LVMH	1743
Microsoft	1972	Roche	1896
Alphabet (Google)	1998	Nestle	1867
Amazon	1994	ASML Holding	1984
Meta (Facebook)	2004	Prosus (Naspers)	1915
Tesla	2003	L'Oreal	1919
Berkshire Hathaway	1962	Novo Nordisk A/S	1923
Nvidia	1993	Accenture (Arthur Andersen)	1913
Visa (Bank Americard)	1958	Novartis AG (Sandoz)	1886
J P Morgan Chase	1799	AstraZeneca	1913

A corporation is deemed to be located in United States or EU based on headquarters location. When a present-day corporation is the result of one or more past merger(s), the founding date refers to the foundation date of the oldest entity, whose name I retained in parentheses.

Impressionistic Evidence Suggesting That Openness to Business Advocacy Promotes Entrepreneurship and Innovation   Hypothesis 1 cannot be tested conclusively because a clean experiment, one where a political system's openness to business advocacy is reduced while everything else stays the same, is not available. However, it is possible to get an impressionistic sense by comparing political systems that are more open to business advocacy with those that are less open. To this end, recall the index mentioned at page 29 that locates industrialized countries on the pluralist-corporatist spectrum. Hypothesis 1 suggests that new and innovative companies should be more successful in pluralist countries than in corporatist countries. In the latter countries, we would expect established incumbents to be more successful.

Table 11.1 provides some impressionistic evidence is favor of Hypothesis 1. The table lists the ten largest companies by capitalization among companies headquartered in the United States versus the European Union (EU), respectively. On inspection, one sees that the largest US companies are much younger (by seventy years, on average) and operate in more innovative sectors, than the largest EU companies. This observation is consistent with Hypothesis 1 because the United States is highly pluralistic while EU countries are generally corporatist.

Hypothesis 1 also suggests that, in more pluralistic countries, regulations should be relatively more friendly toward small and innovative

Pluralistic political systems are easier to do business in

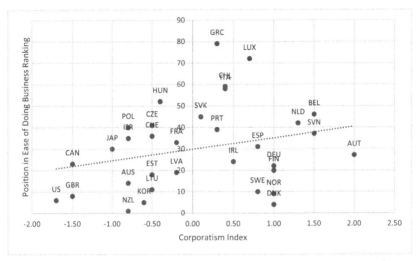

FIGURE 11.1 Correlation between high-income countries' corporatism and position in the World Bank's 2020 Ease of Doing Business ranking (lower value denotes higher rank, i.e., greater ease of doing business). Iceland is missing, because Jahn (2016) does not rate its corporatism level. In less-corporatist countries (those lying on the left side of the graph), it is easier to do business. Analysis produced by the author.

firms than toward large and established ones. The World Bank's "Ease of Doing Business Report" (Eodb) evaluates the pro-business orientation of a country's regulatory system based on a number of features that include: ease of dealing with permits, investor protection, and contract enforcement. I view these features as measuring the degree to which formal protections are available to any firm, small or large. So I make the assumption that a high Eodb ranking benefits small and entrepreneurial firms more than large and established ones, because large and established firms can better protect themselves informally through their influence in the local economy, even if formal protections are low. With this assumption, a higher placement in the Eodb ranking means that regulations are relatively more friendly toward small and entrepreneurial firms than toward large and established ones.

Figure 11.1 plots Jahn's (2016) corporatism index against the country's position in the Eodb ranking. The figure reveals a positive association between pluralism and ease of doing business. This means that a political system's openness to business advocacy correlates with openness to entrepreneurship. This correlation, if interpreted causally, suggests that a political system's openness to business advocacy facilitates business enterprise. Figure 11.1, therefore, suggests that if business advocacy were to be curbed in the United States by making the system more corporatist along European lines, it would become more difficult for small and entrepreneurial firms to succeed in the United States.

Nondemocracies In autocratic political systems, Hypothesis 1 states that no business, be it large or small, unimaginative or innovative, is free to engage in meaningful business advocacy. For example, Uber's disruptive brand of business advocacy would be inconceivable in an autocracy because it would be seen as a direct challenge to political authorities. In China, for example, as soon as the national government announced its intention to regulate ridesharing in 2015, Uber commented: "We are in close communications with local regulators, and will ... follow the spirit of the draft regulation, comply with all requirements, and continuously partner with local governments in implementing the new set of rules."[9]

Note how conciliatory Uber was with Chinese regulators, despite the fact that China's draft rules were very tough: an expert expected them to have a "disastrous impact" on Uber's business.[10] This submissive language was a far cry from Uber's public disparagement of US regulators, whom Kalanick publicly accused of "cronyism" (see page 110). Two weeks after the final rules were issued, Uber announced it would exit China.[11] Yet, throughout this process, Uber never criticized the Chinese regulators.

The generalizable lesson is that business advocacy is more restricted in autocracies than in democracies. Consistent with this observation, Hypothesis 1 states that nondemocratic political systems should give rise to the least-innovation friendly regulations. This prediction is consistent with the so-called "Popper hypothesis,"[12] stating that democracy promotes innovation more than autocracy. Gao et al. (2017) and Wang et al. (2017) provide empirical support for the Popper hypothesis. Of course, there can be many mechanisms, or channels, underlying the Popper hypothesis. The channel I propose is that, when the business sector is unable to advocate for regulatory change, innovation is stifled.

A Caveat This section's case in support of business advocacy is limited by the following caveat. In this section I have used a (cautiously) causal language implying that if, hypothetically, a country moved from

---

[9] Waldmeir (2015).
[10] Waldmeir (2015).
[11] Hinchliffe (2016), Kirby (2016).
[12] Gao et al. (2017).

pluralism to corporatism, or from corporatism to nondemocracy, the innovation-friendliness of regulation would decrease. However, the evidence presented in this section is merely correlational: It is consistent with the causal interpretation, but it does not establish it. There are many confounding factors that vary across countries besides their openness to business advocacy, and the perfect experiment – an exogenous variation in a country's openness to advocacy – is not available.

Learning Points This section addressed the question of whether business advocacy promotes innovation. I addressed this question in the following form: Is there more or less innovation in political systems where business organizations face higher hurdles in advocating with the rule makers? By comparing pluralistic systems where all firms can advocate freely, to corporatist systems where large and established firms can stifle the advocacy of small and innovative firms, to nondemocracies where no firm can advocate freely, I have argued that constraining business advocacy stifles innovation-friendly regulations and, thus, ultimately, innovation.

11.3 CORPORATE ACTIVISM

Mass shootings in the United States have been increasing in frequency and in deadliness.[13] In 2018, the financial sector decided to do something about it.

Minicase 11: Lending bans against firearm manufacturers

In 2018, Bank of America (BoA) decided that it would no longer lend money to firearm manufacturers that produced "military style" weapons for the civilian market. The cause was noble: to reduce mass shootings. Anne Finucane, the bank's vice chairman, said:

We want to contribute in any way we can to reduce these mass shootings. We have had intense conversations over the last few months. And it's our intention not to finance these military-style firearms for civilian use.[a]

Several other large lenders, including Citigroup and JP Morgan, adopted similar policies shortly thereafter.[b]

[a] Alfonseca (2018).
[b] Alfonseca (2018).

[13] Smart and Shell (2021).

This policy shift by the big banks was a well-intentioned move to deal with a serious social problem. It is, also, an example of corporate activism in the sense of the next definition.

Definition 15 (Corporate Activism)   *Corporate activism is a firm's use of its business relationships with customers, suppliers, or workers, in the pursuit of broad social goals not directly tied to its own core business.*

BoA's policy shift in Minicase 11 fits the definition of corporate activism: BoA used its business relationship with customers (refused to lend) in the pursuit of a social goal (reducing mass shootings) that was not directly tied to its own core business (which was to collect money and lend it profitably).

Corporate activism, as defined in Definition 15, is different from business advocacy (Definition 2) in its means (business conduct vs persuasion), its targets (business stakeholders vs government officials), and its proximate goals (societal vs private benefits). For example, consider Uber's efforts to change taxi regulations described at pages 149 and ff. Uber's activities qualify as business advocacy under Definition 2, but not as corporate activism under Definition 15 because its targets were regulators and, also, because Uber was not pursuing a broad social goal beyond its own profits.

Many citizens say they like corporate activism. For example, according to a recent survey, 63 percent of Americans say that "CEOs should step in when the government does not fix societal problems."[14] Interestingly, citizen profess to like corporate activism despite holding a negative view of business advocacy. My interpretation of this dualism is that Americans want corporations to advocate less in their narrow self-interest, and more in the interest of society as a whole. Put differently, citizens understand that corporate activism has the potential to do much good, and they hope that corporations will live up to this potential. However, I argue that corporate activism must be approached with caution. Next, I explain why using Minicase 11 as an example.

Recall that US citizens have quite settled (and sharply divided) preferences regarding firearms regulation. According to the Capitol Hill staffer quoted at page 81: "The two sides have deeply held beliefs that are in complete opposition to one another. ... It's just we're at a stalemate in America. We're very divided. It's pretty much 50/50."

---

[14] 2021 Edelman Trust Barometer.

Seen from the perspective of a citizen who is pro-gun, BoA was going out of its way to unfairly penalize a lawful activity: the production of certain firearms. For these citizens, BoA's corporate activism did not feel like "business fixing a societal problem" but, rather, like a big bank taking sides in a 50–50 political conflict, that is, engaging in partisan politics. This is not to say that, in choosing not to lend to certain firearms producers, BoA was exceeding its prerogatives: one could argue that, as a private company, BoA is free to make operational choices including which businesses it chooses to lend to. I am not taking a position on this argument. Rather, my point is that a sizable fraction of society did not approve of selectively defunding firearms manufacturers merely because of what they produced. Equally, a sizable fraction of society was in favor of defunding the industry. In short, the issue was a partisan one.

Broadening the focus beyond the specifics of Minicase 11, there is reason to be concerned about the blurry boundary between corporate activism and partisan politics. This is because, besides corporate activism, there exists the ordinary political process. If a social policy is preferred by more than 50 percent of the population, the ordinary political process is expected to turn this policy into law without the need for corporate activism. The concern, then, is that whatever causes are left for corporate activists to champion are precisely those causes that are supported by less than 50 percent of the population. This is not to say, of course, that corporate activism is always problematic: it is true, after all, that at any point in time some popular policies may not be enshrined in law due to frictions in the political process. When these frictions are large, corporate advocacy can play a valuable role. However, as a matter of logic, we must be cognizant that, if democratic institutions work reasonably well and, at the same time, there is a lot of corporate activism, then there is a nontrivial chance that some of the activism may inadvertently shade into partisan politics.

The second reason why corporations should consider carefully before engaging in corporate activism as characterized in Definition 15 is that, to the extent that the activism focuses on broad social goals beyond the scope of the firm's core business, the activist corporation engages in subjects in which it has no unique expertise. Thus, for example, in Minicase 11, BoA did not have unique expertise in the social costs and benefits of different types of firearms. Therefore, BoA did not have much knowledge to add to the firearms regulation debate. This is in sharp contrast with business advocacy, where the firm typically operates within its own business sectors and, therefore, can bring to the table its private knowledge of technology in a way that, potentially, improves social welfare.[15] This channel of welfare improvement is less likely to be present in corporate activism.

The third consideration is a practical one. When a corporation ventures into public policy beyond the perimeter of its narrow business interest, its mission morphs subtly, but distinctly. Its brand effectively expands beyond its core product or service and comes to include public policy. The expanded brand risks becoming vulnerable to public pressure by loud, but potentially fringe societal groups, and then to counteraction by political institutions. In the end, the corporation risks becoming both a political forum and a target of political actors. For an example of counteraction by political institutions, in 2021 the state of Texas passed a law that barred companies that "discriminate against the firearms or ammunition industries" from doing business with the state.[16] The law was targeted against BoA, Citigroup, and JP Morgan, the big banks that had previously boycotted gun manufacturers (see Minicase 11). As a result, these banks were forced to forfeit the lucrative municipal bond underwriting business in Texas. This is not to say, of course, that the big banks should not have engaged in corporate activism. After all, the banks themselves were likely facing pressures by anti-gun activists. Moreover, many employees probably felt good about boycotting certain firearm manufacturers. Finally, a paternalistic argument could be made that fewer firearms are good for people, regardless of how people feel about the issue. The point still stands, however, that political actors made the big banks pay a price for their activism.

In this section I have made the case that corporate activism, while sometimes unambiguously prosocial, should be approached with caution by business corporations.

Learning Points   Corporate activism has the potential to do much good. However, when traditional political channels operate reasonably well, there is a risk that corporate activism can shade into partisan political activity. When the firm becomes a partisan player, it exposes itself to political pressures. Therefore, corporate activism should be approached with caution by business corporations.

---

[15] For example, as I described at pages 149 and ff. Uber knew of a better way to transport riders from point A to point B. This knowledge represented Uber's private information that could, and in the event arguably did, improve social welfare.

[16] Dizard (2021).

11.4 TAKEAWAYS FROM THIS CHAPTER

The general public views business advocacy with suspicion. Should business advocacy be restricted? No, I have argued. Economic theory suggests that restricting the ability of business to communicate with government officials will decrease the officials' ability to make accurate decisions, without making their decisions any more independent. Furthermore, the business sector has an enormous amount of information to contribute to the policy making process: Business advocacy that results in pro-innovation regulations can have huge social value. I have argued that if business advocacy is easy and transparent, small and innovative companies have the chance to shape regulations in a way that increases innovation. When business advocacy is made more difficult, small and innovative companies are likely to be disproportionately affected, and established incumbents are likely to benefit in comparison, creating the risk that regulations are used to stifle innovation.

Corporate activism, as defined in Definition 15, is different from business advocacy in its means, targets, and proximate goals. Despite being well intentioned, popular with public opinion, and sometimes prosocial, corporate activism should be approached cautiously by business corporations.

12

Competitive Strategy versus SBM

This chapter compares and contrasts SBM with Competitive Strategy (CS). The aim is to situate SBM in relation to CS in the space of ideas.

SBM and CS share the same ultimate goal: to protect and increase long-term firm value. But, though the ultimate goal is the same, the two disciplines differ in the following dimensions:

1. **Origins of the Threat to Firm Value** In Porter's canonical "five forces" account, CS deals with five threats to value creation and capture, all of which come from *market agents*: either competitors or customers or suppliers. In SBM, by contrast, the threat to firm value is a change in the rules of the competitive game, and it comes from *nonmarket agents*: legislatures and regulators.

2. **Managerial Mindset** Operating in the CS arena requires a different mindset and strategic toolkit from the one required to operate in the SBM arena.

3. **Strategic Constraints** CS takes the rules of the competitive game as given and gives strategic prescriptions *within* those rules. SBM is concerned with the making of the rules, and gives prescriptions about how to change them.

4. **Vulnerabilities** In CS, a firm needs to be different and uniquely situated in order to "win the competitive game." In SBM, a firm needs many similarly situated coalition partners in order to "win the rules of the game."

5. **Behavior That Is Deemed Unlawful** In the market arena, monetary transfers are lawful (e.g., through prices or contracts) but coordination among firms is deemed illegal (cartel behavior). In the

politico-regulatory arena, certain monetary transfers (e.g., through bribes) are deemed illegal but coordination among firms is lawful (e.g., ad hoc coalition formation, trade associations).

The rest of the chapter illustrates these differences using examples and a theoretical model.

12.1 DIFFERENT ORIGIN OF THREATS TO FIRM VALUE

Michael Porter's canonical account of CS highlights five threats to the firm's profitability. They are:

1. Threat of new entrants
2. Threat of a substitute product
3. Increase in the customers' bargaining power
4. Increase in the suppliers' bargaining power
5. Increase in the competitive rivalry among existing firms

All these threats originate from *market forces*, including technological change. In SBM, instead, the threat to profits originate from forces beyond the market, namely, from the *statutory power of elected officials and regulators*. This threat is not contemplated in Porter's framework. For example, the threat to the recycling industry featured in Section 2.2 is not really captured by any of Porter's five forces – it doesn't comfortably slot into the CS framework.

Learning Points In CS, the threats to value creation and capture originate from market forces, including innovation. In SBM, they originate from the political process.

12.2 DIFFERENT MANAGERIAL MINDSET

From the perspective of a CEO or general manager, the mindset and toolkit of CS are quite different from those of SBM. The following examples illustrate this point.

- **Recyclers Case of Section 2.2** The recyclers were getting hit with ruinous Superfund cleanup fees. In this predicament, what might the CS mindset and toolkit prescribe? Perhaps, something like this: Look for additional capital to pay for the cleanup charges so that your business can survive the financial hit while some of your competitors go bankrupt. Then, use whatever market power you have gained from the industry shakeout to increase your margins and, hopefully, compensate those who provided the capital injection. The

SBM prescription, in contrast, was for the recyclers to get involved in politics and lobby to get the Superfund law amended – which they did.

- **Pink Viagra Case of Section 2.7** The CS mindset would be, presumably, to improve the safety and effectiveness of the drug. Of course, this may not have been technically feasible, or economical. The approach taken by the company, instead, was to pressure regulators in the court of public opinion, and nudge them into approving the drug.[1]
- **Uber's Service Being Illegal** Before Uber was made legal, local taxi regulations required for-hire drivers to own a taxi license. The CS prescription to enter the taxi market might, perhaps, have involved purchasing taxi licenses and assigning them to Uber drivers. This would have required a large capital outlay and, arguably, would have totally changed Uber's business model. The SBM prescription, instead, was for Uber to seek the repeal of the license requirements – which Uber effectively accomplished.

These examples illustrate that CS and SBM represent different domains of managerial activity. In these examples, the CS mindset and toolkit were not likely to help the CEOs overcome their challenges. Instead, the CEO's attention needed to be pointed in a different direction, and different expertise was required – to wit, SBM.

Learning Points CS and SBM represent different domains of managerial activity requiring distinct mindsets and toolkits.

12.3 DIFFERENT SET OF STRATEGIC CONSTRAINTS

According to David Baron, the founder of SBM as an academic field, CS and SBM differ in the following way:

Competitive analysis typically takes the rules of the game — the regulatory system, for example — as given, whereas the nonmarket strategy perspective views these rules as endogenous and hence the focus of strategy.[2]

Baron's quote indicates that CS and SBM operate under different strategic constraints. CS takes the rules of the *competitive game* as given, and

---

[1] I stop short of saying that this is the SBM prescription, because SBM must be deployed ethically, and one could question the ethics of the Addyi campaign.
[2] Baron (1995).

operates within those rules. SBM, in contrast, does not take the rules of the competitive game as fixed constraints: Rather, it seeks to shape them by advocating within the rules of the *political game*.

Learning Points CS takes the rules of the *competitive game* as given, and operates within those rules. SBM, in contrast, seeks to shape these rules by operating within the rules of the *political game*.

12.4 DIFFERENT VULNERABILITIES

In CS, a firm is vulnerable if it loses its uniqueness, that is, if its product or its ability to bargain with customers or suppliers become commoditized. In SBM, by contrast, uniqueness actually represents a vulnerability. An obvious manifestation of this basic principle is antitrust enforcement: a firm that manages to dominate its market has achieved the ultimate goal of CS. But then, having become a monopolist, the firm is vulnerable to antitrust regulation. The point is that uniqueness is a strength in CS, but a vulnerability in SBM. This principle applies more broadly than just to antitrust enforcement: This section illustrates the principle within a theoretical example in which a firm is at risk of a potential regulation. Within this example, we will show that whereas uniqueness is the source of success in CS, it puts the firm at risk of emergent regulation and, therefore, of SBM failure.

A Theoretical Example Next, I provide a theoretical example in which each of Porter's five forces are introduced individually. All five forces will be shown to reduce to a single principle: diminished uniqueness. This exercise will illustrate the fundamental principle recorded in Theorem 4: Uniqueness is the source of success in CS.

Minicase 12: Theoretical example

- **Supply:** There is a single retailer which can produce up to two identical objects at a cost of $1 each.
- **Demand:** There are three identical consumers, each with unit demand and valuation equal to $1.3.

This minicase describes a setting where a single retailer can produce up to two units of a product at a unit cost of 1, and each consumer is willing to pay up to $1.3 to get one unit but has no value for a second unit. In this setting, the equilibrium price is $p = \$1.3$ regardless of whether the firm behaves as a price taker or monopolistically. At this price, both items get traded so the social value created by the market exchange is $2 \cdot \$0.3 = \$0.6$.

Note that the firm extracts all the surplus in the economy, and buyers are left with zero surplus. This is because what the firm produces is *scarce*: There are three consumers and at most two items, so demand exceeds supply. In this sense, it can be said that the firm's product is "unique."

CS in the Theoretical Example Within the context of Minicase 12, Porter's five forces can be understood as pointing to a *loss of uniqueness*. Let's see why this is so for each of the five forces.

1. **Threat of New Entrants** A second identical firm to the incumbent enters the market, bringing the total number of items available for sale to four. Now, the only competitive price that clears the market is $p = \$1$ and, after entry, both sellers make zero profits. Intuitively, the incumbent's profits decrease because, relative to Minicase 12, the incumbent has become *less unique*.

2. **Threat of Substitute Product** An imperfect substitute, let's call it a "copycat" product, is invented that is valued at $\$1.2$ by the three consumers, and is supplied by a competitive sector in any amount at the price of $\$1.1$. In the original product market, the price is now $\$1.2$ or less. Relative to Minicase 12, the invention of the copycat product reduces the original seller's profits *because the copycat product replicate the original product*, albeit imperfectly.

3. **Increase in the Bargaining Power of Customers** All the buyers join together and form a cooperative in order to exercise market power. The cooperative imposes a take-it-or-leave-it price $p = \$1 + \varepsilon$, with ε a very small positive number. The seller is forced to accept. Then the buyer's surplus increases and the seller's profits collapse, relative to Minicase 12. Profits collapse because, by merging into a single entity, the customers have become *more unique*, or, put differently, the firm has become *less unique relative to its customers*.

4. **Increase in the Bargaining Power of Suppliers** Suppose that, rather than having at most two items for sale, the retailer can now purchase any number of items from a competitive wholesale sector at a price of $\$1$, and re-sell them to the customer. Now, the competitive retail price in the product market is $\$1$ and the monopoly retail price is $\$1.3$. If the wholesalers increase their market power by merging into a single entity (or, equivalently, operating as a cartel), they can bargain with the retailer from a position of strength and

raise the wholesale price above $1, which reduces the retailer's profits. Again, the uniqueness principle holds: The wholesalers' surplus is increased, and the retailer's decreased, when many small wholesalers aggregate into a single entity, thereby making themselves *more unique* (in this case, what matters is the relative uniqueness of the wholesalers vis-à-vis the retailer).

5. **Increase in the Competitive Rivalry among Existing Firms** Consider the setting in part 1, and imagine that the two firms merge so that they become a monopoly. Such a monopolist owns four items. The best strategy for the post-merger monopolist is to withhold one item and sell the other three at a price of $1.3 each. Total industry profits are $0.9, which is higher than pre-merger industry profits ($0). Again, we see that by becoming *more unique* (from two firms to a single one), firms benefit.

The above analysis is intended to illustrate that all of Porter's five forces are, from a firm's perspective, manifestation of a single underlying risk: the risk of *diminished uniqueness*.[3] This notion is expressed in the following fundamental theorem.

Theorem 4 (Fundamental Theorem of CS) *In a market environment, a firm's ability to make profits and capture value is threatened when the firm's contribution to social surplus becomes less unique.*

This theorem says that, in CS, a firm needs to be different and unique in order to "win the competitive game."

SBM in Minicase 12 In Minicase 12, intuitively, the risk of regulation is high: Customers do not benefit at all from trading, so these same customers, acting as voters, will attempt to use regulation to improve their welfare. What features of the environment increase or decrease the probability of regulation? In what follows, I show that the answer depends on who owns the firm. The general principle that I seek to illustrate is that the *distribution of value* is critical in SBM, in a way that it isn't in CS. In addition, the firm's owners have a greater probability of beyond-market success if they are *similarly situated* to a large set of agents in society.

---

[3] The idea that profits are the reward to unique contributions to social value has been developed by many economists, going back at least to Adam Smith. The present treatment is inspired by the work of Joseph Ostroy, a professor of economics at UCLA.

The next minicase builds on the structure in Minicase 12 by specifying who owns the firm, an issue which was not relevant for the CS analysis. I also assume that the regulation is determined by a legislature, and that all consumers are voters. I must, finally, take a stand on the form of regulation. In the real world, regulation can take many forms; here, to fix ideas, I assume that regulation takes the form of price controls. This implies that the price p is not set by the market but, rather, by elected officials.

Minicase 13: Adding regulation to Minicase 12

In the setting of Minicase 12, assume that every consumer is also a voter. Suppose the price p is set not by the market, but by an elected official who maximizes the welfare of a majority, that is, at least two out of the three consumers/voters.

What is the regulated price in this environment? This depends on the distribution of the value created by the firm. Next, I examine two polar cases.

1. **All the Shares Are Owned by a Single Consumer.** If all the shares are owned by Citizen 1 (the "capitalist"), then the other two citizens (the two "proletarians") receive no dividends. If the price is capped at $p = \$1$, I assume that rationing is accomplished by randomly allocating among the three citizens the rights to purchase the two goods. Under the price cap the firm makes no profits, so Citizen 1's expected surplus (inclusive of dividends) is only $(2/3) \cdot \$0.3 = \$0.2$, compared with $\$0.6$ under the unregulated equilibrium price $p = \$1.3$. Each of the other two citizens' expected surplus is $(2/3) \cdot \$0.3$ under the regulated price, compared with $\$0$ at the unregulated price. Since a majority of the voters prefers $p = \$1$, the politician will enact regulation to cap the price at $\$1$. This is the strictest possible level of price regulation at which the firm is still willing to produce and sell. Figure 12.1a depicts this scenario.

2. **Two Voters Each Own Half of the Firm.** If Citizens 1 and 2 each own half of the firm, their expected surplus at the regulated price is $(2/3) \cdot \$0.3 = \$0.2$ each, compared with $(1/2) \cdot \$0.6 = \$0.3$ each at the unregulated price. Therefore these two citizens prefer no regulation. The third voter (the proletarian) receives an expected surplus of $(2/3) \cdot \$0.3$ at the regulated price, compared with $\$0$

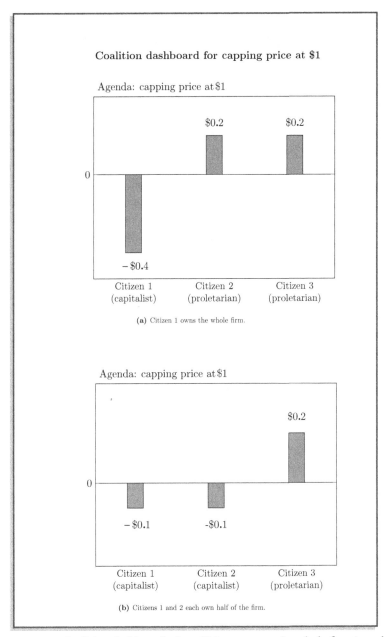

FIGURE 12.1 Coalition dashboard when Citizen 1 owns the whole firm (panel a) and when Citizens 1 and 2 each own half of the firm (panel b). Status quo is the unregulated price, $p = \$1.3$.

at the unregulated price. Since a majority of the voters (the two capitalists) strictly prefer no regulation, the politician will not regulate the price, and the price will coincide with the market price in Minicase 12. Figure 12.1b depicts this scenario.

Figure 12.1 depicts the coalition dashboard for each case. The dollar figures associated with each bar represent the change in expected surplus, inclusive of dividends, relative to the status quo, if the Agenda is enacted. All the bars have the same color value because all citizens are assumed to have the same influence. In panel (a) a majority favors regulating the price. In panel (b), a majority favors the unregulated price.

Comparing panels (a) and (b) shows that the allocation of ownership and profits plays a key role in determining the threat of regulation. This is because the *distribution of value* is critical in SBM, in a way that it isn't in CS. In fact, no information about firm ownership was even needed to carry out the CS analysis. Note, also, the language shift: I referred to consumers as voters because, from the perspective of SBM, consumers are also voters.

A second important theme emerges from the analysis of Minicase 13: The firm is better protected from regulation if its owners' interests align with those of a large coalition. We see this because regulation is friendlier to the firm when its ownership is broadly shared, than when it is narrowly held. This observation, of course, is a manifestation of the fact that large coalitions are helpful in SBM. The lessons from the analysis of Minicase 13 are summarized in the following theorem.

Theorem 5 (Fundamental Theorem of SBM) *In the beyond-market environment, the regulatory threat to a firm's ability to make profits depends on the allocation of the surplus generated by the firm. Profits are at greater risk of expropriation when the surplus is narrowly rather than broadly distributed.*

This result illustrates the difference between SBM and CS. In SBM, the allocation of ownership and profits is critical for determining the threats to the firm (Theorem 5). In CS, in contrast, the allocation of ownership and profits does not matter (Theorem 4). Furthermore, those who own the profits have a greater probability of beyond-market success if they are *similarly situated* to a large set of agents in society.

Learning Points   Value distribution does not matter in CS, but it matters a great deal in SBM. In CS, uniqueness is the key to market success. In

SBM, being similarly situated to a large set of agents is key to regulatory success.

12.5 DIFFERENT FIRM BEHAVIORS ARE DEEMED UNLAWFUL

In the market arena, antitrust law prohibits cartels that fix prices or restrict output. Thus, the rules of the competitive game forbid coordinated collective action in the domain of prices or quantities. In the politico-regulatory arena, by contrast, firms are allowed to coordinate on advocacy. Ad hoc coalitions and trade associations, for example – the analogue of a cartel – are a form of coordinated collective action that is not only legal but, often, encouraged. The only limitation is that the coordination must not involve prices or quantities.

The next case illustrates a case of open cooperation in the politico-regulatory arena.

Minicase 14: Lawful cooperation in the beyond-market arena

Microsoft and Google have long battled each other, including in the regulatory arena. Prior to 2016, Microsoft had worked with EU regulators to support the regulators' case to limit Google's search dominance. From an internal Microsoft division called "Office of Strategic Relations," lobbyists and attorneys had supported interest groups and companies opposed to Google, including supporting their lawsuits against Google.[a] Conversely, Google had supported the EU regulators' case against Microsoft's practice of bundling the Internet Explorer browser with the Windows operating system.[b]

In 2016, the two companies decided to bury the hatchet and agreed to cooperate in the regulatory arena. According to a Google spokesperson:

we've now agreed to withdraw regulatory complaints against one another.

As part of this agreement, the two companies withdrew twenty patent-infringement lawsuits against each other, and Microsoft left two industry groups that lobbied against Google.

[a] Tilley and Tracy (2022).
[b] This minicase is based on Greene and Nicas (2016).

The point of this minicase is that explicit cooperation is lawful in the beyond-market arena. By contrast, in the market arena it would have been illegal for Microsoft and Google to coordinate on quantities or prices. On the other hand, in the market arena the exchange of money between firms, or between firms and customers, is not problematic. In the beyond-market arena, in contrast, paying money to government officials is not allowed.

In sum, CS and SBM operate under such different set of rules, that the type of firm behaviors that are deemed unlawful are almost diametrically opposed.

Learning Points   Coordination among firms is illegal in the market arena but encouraged in the beyond-market arena. In the market arena, monetary payments among market actors are legal, but in the beyond-market arena monetary payments to government officials are illegal.

12.6 TAKEAWAYS FROM THIS CHAPTER

Despite sharing the same ultimate goal, which is to increase firm value, CS and SBM differ fundamentally. The tools of CS are product and price; the tool of SBM is advocacy. Being unique is an advantage in CS, not so in SBM: In SBM, a firm needs many similarly situated coalition partners in order to "win the rules of the game." Coordination among firms is illegal in CS, encouraged in SBM.

Glossary

Agents People or organizations who can act in the beyond-market arena. The actions include: voting, protesting, advocating, creating coalitions, and sharing information.

Appointed official A government official who is hired by another government official, as opposed to being elected by the public. For example, a biologist who works for the Environmental Protection Agency, or an economist who works at the Treasury department.

Bill The text of a law that has been introduced, but not yet been voted on and approved. In the United States, most bills never get voted on.[1]

Business/corporation/firm These terms are used interchangeably.

Constituents The citizens who have the right to elect a specific representative are called the representative's constituents.

Elected official A government official who is elected by the public, as opposed to being appointed by another official: for example, a member of the US Congress. Legislators and some executive positions (such as the US president, or state governors) are elected officials. Elected officials are motivated by the prospect of reelection or election to higher office. Chapter 4 deals with elected officials.

Government official Someone who performs a governmental function. Includes appointed and elected officials.

Institution The legislature or regulator with jurisdiction over a given Issue.

Interests (also commonly referred to as members of an interest group). This term refers to agents who are affected by a given Issue.

---

[1] About 95 percent of the bills, amounting to about 5,000 a year, are introduced and never even receive a vote. See www.govtrack.us/congress/bills/statistics.

Issue A change in the rules of the competitive game, i.e., a change in the laws or regulations that govern economic activity.

Law A rule that is issued by a legislature (elected body).

Legislator A government official whose function is to vote on bills which, if approved, become laws.

Policy agenda The change in the business-relevant laws and regulations that a business advocates for or against. Very similar to an Issue.

Policy entrepreneur A person, or organization, who advocates for a policy agenda.

Regulation A rule that is issued by a regulator (appointed official).

Regulator A government official whose job is to write implementing regulations (such as technical standards) for existing laws, to monitor compliance with the laws, and sometimes to impose penalties for noncompliance. Regulators are appointed, not elected. Most regulators are appointed by other regulators and have strong job security. A few top regulators are appointed by elected officials and serve at their pleasure, meaning that they can be replaced at any time. Chapter 7 deals with regulators.

Rules of the competitive game Laws and regulations that control value creation and capture. They include taxes, subsidies, compliance rules, production and marketability standards, licensing requirements, and many other rules besides.

References

2021 Edelman Trust Barometer. www.edelman.com/sites/g/files/aatuss191/files/2021-03/2021%20Edelman%20Trust%20Barometer.pdf

Acton Institute (2022) "The Overton Window with Joseph Lehman." March 2, 2022. YouTube www.youtube.com/watch?v=-QVB3EwOUC8

Alfonseca, Kiara (2018, April 11) "Bank of America stops financing for makers of 'military style' rifles." NBC News Online. www.nbcnews.com/news/us-news/bank-america-stops-financing-makers-military-style-rifles-n865106

Allahrakha, Meraj, et al. (2019) "The effects of the Volcker Rule on corporate bond trading: Evidence from the underwriting exemption." OFR Working paper 19-02. www.financialresearch.gov/working-papers/files/OFRwp-19-02_the-effects-of-the-volcker-rule-on-corporate-bond-trading.pdf

Ansolabehere, Stephen, John M. de Figueiredo, and James M. Snyder Jr. (2003) "Why is there so little money in U.S. politics?" *Journal of Economic Perspectives* 17(1): 105–30.

Austin, Scott Chris Canipe and Sarah Slobin (2019) "The billion dollar startup club." The Wall Street Journal. First published Feb. 18, 2015, updated up to Sept. 2019. Accessed Jan 23, 2022. www.wsj.com/graphics/billion-dollar-club/

Balfour, David JK, Neal L. Benowitz, Suzanne M. Colby, Dorothy K. Hatsukami, Harry A. Lando, Scott J. Leischow, Caryn Lerman et al. "Balancing consideration of the risks and benefits of e-cigarettes." *American Journal of Public Health* 111, no. 9 (2021): 1661–1672.

Bank Policy Institute (2020) "Beware the Kraken" BPI Staff, published online on October 21, 2020 https://bpi.com/beware-the-kraken/

Banuri, Sheheryar, Stefan Dercon, and Varun Gauri (2019). "Biased policy professionals." The World Bank Economic Review 33(2): 310–327.

Barry, Keith (2020) "Leaving consumers in the dark." Consumer Report, August 31, 2020. www.consumerreports.org/car-safety/some-cars-will-never-be-crash-tested-crash-test-ratings/

Battaglini, Marco (2002) "Multiple referrals and multidimensional cheap talk." *Econometrica* 70.4: 1379–1401.

Baumgartner, Frank R., Jeffrey M. Berry, Marie Hojnacki, Beth L. Leech, and David C. Kimball. (2009). *Lobbying and policy change.* Chicago: University of Chicago Press.

Beer, Jeff (2017) "How NRA advertising changed the second amendment-and American gun culture" Fast Company, published 10-06-17 www.fast company.com/40477572/how-nra-advertising-changed-the-second-amen dment-and-american-gun-culture

Beland, Daniel and Michael Howlett (2016) "The role and impact of the multiple-streams approach in comparative policy analysis." *Journal of Comparative Policy Analysis: Research and Practice* 18(3), 221–227.

Benzkofer, Stephan "When a Chicago police censor ruled over films with an iron fist." *Chicago Tribune*, Feb. 20, 2015.

Bertrand, Marianne, Matilde Bombardini, and Francesco Trebbi (2014) "Is it whom you know or what you know? An empirical assessment of the lobbying process." *American Economic Review* 104(12): 3885–3920.

Berman, Jillian (2018) "How the Great Recession turned America's student-loan problem into a $1.5 trillion crisis." Marketwatch, Published online: Oct. 7, 2018. www.marketwatch.com/story/3-ways-the-great-recession-turned-ameri cas-student-loan-problem-into-a-crisis-2018-09-06

Black, Gregory D. (1989) "Hollywood censored: The production code administration and the Hollywood film industry, 1930–1940." *Film History* 3(3): 167–189.

Block, Jennifer and Liz canner (2016) "The 'Grassroots Campaign' for 'Female Viagra' was actually funded by its manufacturer." The Cut, Sept. 8, 2016. www .thecut.com/2016/09/how-addyi-the-female-viagra-won-fda-approval.html

Board of Governors of the Federal Reserve System (2021) "Economic well-being of U.S. households in 2020," May 2021. www.federalreserve.gov/ publications/files/2020-report-economic-well-being-us-households-202105.pdf

Bombardini, Matilde, and Francesco Trebbi (2020) "Empirical models of lobby-ing." *Annual Review of Economics* 12: 391–413.

Brady, David W. (2014) "Sure, Congress is polarized. But other legis-latures are more so." The Washington Post, posted on February 17, 2014 at 4:55 p.m. EST at www.washingtonpost.com/news/monkey-cage/ wp/2014/02/17/sure-congress-is-polarized-but-other-legislatures-are-more-so/

Branch, Anthony D. (2018). "National Traffic and Motor Vehicle Safety Act." Encyclopedia Britannica, 16 Mar. 2018.

Bräuninger, Thomas, and Marc Debus (2009) "Legislative agenda-setting in par-liamentary democracies." *European Journal of Political Research* 48.6 (2009): 804–839.

Brenan, Megan (2021) "Americans' Trust in Media Dips to Second Lowest on Record" Gallup October 7, 2021 https://news.gallup.com/poll/355526/ americans-trust-media-dips-second-lowest-record.aspx www.britannica.com/ topic/National-Traffic-and-Motor-Vehicle-Safety-Act. Accessed 24 January 2022.

Brodwin Erin (2019) "The FDA just called out e-cig startup Juul and tobacco giant Altria for backing away from a pledge to fight teen vaping." Business Insider, Feb 8, 2019, 10:02 AM.

Bush, George W. (2008) "Memorandum on Modification of the Withdrawal of Areas of the United States Outer Continental Shelf From Leasing Disposition" July 14, 2008. Online by Gerhard Peters and John T. Woolley, The American Presidency Project. www.presidency.ucsb.edu/node/278019

Carpenter, Daniel (2014). *Reputation and power*. Princeton University Press, 2014.

Carpenter, Daniel, and David A. Moss, eds. (2014). *Preventing regulatory capture: Special interest influence and how to limit it*. Cambridge University Press, 2014.

Carrigan, Christopher (2014). "Captured by disaster? Reinterpreting regulatory behavior in the shadow of the Gulf oil spill." In *Preventing regulatory capture: Special interest influence and how to limit it* Carpenter, Daniel, and David A. Moss, eds. (2014): 239–291.

Cassidy, John (2010) "The Volcker Rule: Obama's economic adviser and his battles over the financial-reform bill." *The New Yorker*, 26(10).

Congressional Research Service (2022) "Membership of the 117th Congress: A Profile." Congressional Research Service R46705 Updated March 31, 2022 https://crsreports.congress.gov/product/pdf/R/R46705

Constine, Josh (2012) "SOPA Protests Sway Congress: 31 Opponents Yesterday, 122 Now." TechCrunch, January 19, 2012, 6:37 PM MST. https://techcrunch.com/2012/01/19/sopa-opponents-supporters/

Corliss, Richard (2007) "What Jack Valenti Did for Hollywood." Time Magazine, Apr. 27, 2007. http://content.time.com/time/arts/article/0,8599, 1615388,00.html

Cowley, Stacy and Tara Siegel Bernard (2022) "Navient agrees to cancel 66,000 student borrowers' loans to settle claims of predatory lending." *The New York Times*, Jan. 13, 2022.

Crawford, Vincent P., and Joel Sobel (9182) "Strategic Information Transmission." *Econometrica*, 50 (no. 6, 1982): 1431—51.

De Loecker, Jan, and Jan Eeckhout (2021). "Global market power." Manuscript, 10 February, 2021 www.janeeckhout.com/wp-content/uploads/Global.pdf.

Dengler, Ralph S.J. (1979) "The First Screen Kiss and 'The Cry of Censorship'," *Journal of Popular Film and Television* 7(3): 267–272.

De Waal, Frans BM. (1996). *Good natured: The origins of right and wrong in humans and other animals*. Harvard University Press, 1996.

Diermeier, Daniel, Herschel Cutler, and Jonathan Cutler (2017). "Recyclers v. Superfund (A-D): The Politics of 'Unintended Consequences'." Kellogg School of Management Cases 5-104-022(A-D).

Dizard, John (2021) "Texas showdown shows limits of seeking gun control through banks." Financial Times, October 29, 2021 www.ft.com/content/ 06e17034-23d5-4fd5-8583-b40c069545ea

Farrell, Diana, Fiona Greig, and Erica Deadman. (2019) "Student Loan Payments: Evidence from 4 Million Families" JPMorgan Chase Institute. www .jpmorganchase.com/corporate/institute/student-loan-payments-report.htm.

FDA News Release (2019) "Trump Administration Combating Epidemic of Youth E-Cigarette Use with Plan to Clear Market of Unauthorized, Non-Tobacco-Flavored E-Cigarette Products." September 11, 2019. www.fda .gov/news-events/press-announcements/trump-administration-combating-epidemic-youth-e-cigarette-use-plan-clear-market-unauthorized-non

FDA (2020) "Vaporizers, E-Cigarettes, and other Electronic Nicotine Delivery Systems (ENDS)." www.fda.gov/tobacco-products/products-ingredients-components/vaporizers-e-cigarettes-and-other-electronic-nicotine-delivery-systems-ends

Fowler, Anthony, Haritz Garro, and Jörg L. Spenkuch (2020) "Quid pro quo? corporate returns to campaign contributions." *The Journal of Politics* 82.3 (2020): 844–858.

Gaetano, Chris (2019) "Regulators Exempt Small Banks from Volcker Rule." The Trusted Professional, July 10, 2019. www.nysscpa.org/news/publications/the-trusted-professional/article/regulators-exempt-small-banks-from-volcker-rule-071019.

Gallup (2022) "Tobacco and Smoking" webpage, https://news.gallup.com/poll/1717/Tobacco-Smoking.aspx accessed 2-21-2022.

Gao, Yanyan, Leizhen Zang, Antoine Roth, and Puqu Wang (2017) "Does democracy cause innovation? An empirical test of the popper hypothesis." *Research Policy* 46, no. 7 (2017): 1272–1283.

Gilson, Dave (2013) "This Collection of NRA Ads Reveals Its Descent Into Crazy." Mother Jones, published April 10, 2013, www.motherjones.com/politics/2013/04/national-rifle-association-ads-history/

Gitlen, Jeff (2022) "A Look Into the History of Student Loans" Lendedu.com, published online on January 19, 2022 https://lendedu.com/blog/history-of-student-loans

Graham, J., Haidt, J., Koleva, S., Motyl, M., Iyer, R., Wojcik, S. P., and Ditto, P. H. (2013). "Moral foundations theory: The pragmatic validity of moral pluralism." In *Advances in experimental social psychology* (Vol. 47, pp. 55–130). Academic Press.

Greene, Jay and Jack Nicas "Microsoft, Google End Regulatory Disputes." The Wall Street Journal, April 22, 2016 7:14 pm ET, www.wsj.com/articles/microsoft-withdraws-complaints-to-regulators-about-google-1461333788?mod=article_inline

Grossman, Sanford J. (1981) "The informational role of warranties and private disclosure about product quality." *The Journal of Law and Economics* 24.3 (1981): 461–483.

Gutowski, Stephen (2021) "Why Can't Democrats Pass Gun Control?" The Atlantic, September 24, 2021 www.theatlantic.com/ideas/archive/2021/09/nra-broken-so-why-cant-democrats-pass-gun-control/620190/

Haidt, Jonathan. (2012). *The righteous mind: Why good people are divided by politics and religion.* Vintage, 2012.

Haidt, Jonathan, and Craig Joseph (2004) "Intuitive ethics: How innately prepared intuitions generate culturally variable virtues." *Daedalus* 133.4 (2004): 55–66.

Hall, Richard L., and Alan V. Deardorff (2006) "Lobbying as legislative subsidy." *American Political Science Review* 100.1 (2006): 69–84.

Hanania, Richard (2017) "The personalities of politicians: A big five survey of American legislators." *Personality and Individual Differences* 108 (2017): 164–167.

Helhoski, Anna (2021) "What would it take to solve the student debt crisis?" Associated Press, published online on May 26, 2021 https://apnews.com/article/lifestyle-business-985cd1e840698acd547d5032764a5c68

Herrnson, Paul S., and Jennifer A. Heerwig (2021). "The Super Women and the Super Men behind Super PACs: The Emergence of a New Source of Inequality in Campaign Financing." Manuscript.

Hinchliffe, Emma (2016) "Uber is now legal in China, but drivers have to play by a new set of rules" Mashable, published July 28, 2016. https://mashable.com/article/uber-legal-china

Hofland, P. (2013) "Reversal of Fortune: How a Vilified Drug Became a Life-saving Agent in the 'War' Against Cancer," Onco'Zine. Published November 30, 2013. https://oncozine.com/reversal-of-fortune-how-a-vilified-drug-became-a-life-saving-agentin-the-war-against-cancer/.

Hogenmiller, Alycia, Alessandra Hirsch and Adriane Fugh-Berman (2017) "The Score is Even." The Hastings Center weblog, published On: June 14, 2017. www.thehastingscenter.org/the-score-is-even/

Hrynovsky, Zach and Megan Brenan (2022) "What Percentage of Americans Vape?" Gallup News, https://news.gallup.com/poll/267413/percentage-americans-vape.aspx accessed 2-21-2022.

Hurst, Clifford G. (2008). "Sustainable telemarketing? A new theory of consumer behavior." *Direct Marketing: An International Journal*.

IIHS (2022) "About our tests." www.iihs.org/ratings/about-our-tests, accessed Jan 24, 2022.

Jahn, Detlef (2016) "Changing of the guard: trends in corporatist arrangements in 42 highly industrialized societies from 1960 to 2010." Socio-Economic Review, Volume 14, Issue 1, January 2016, pp. 47–71.

Kaplan, Sheila (2021) "Juul Is Fighting to Keep Its E-Cigarettes on the U.S. Market." *The New York Times*, Published July 5, 2021 Updated Oct. 12, 2021.

Keil, Richard (1995) "Nra Apologizes For 'Jack Boot' Letter" The Seattle Times, May 18, 1995 https://archive.seattletimes.com/archive/?date=19950518&slug=2121718

Kiel, Paul, and Dan Nguyen (2021) "Bailout Tracker" ProPublica, Published online on April 15, 2009, updated August 30, 2021; available at https://projects.propublica.org/bailout/list.

Kingdon, J. W. (1984). *Agendas, Alternatives and Public Policies*. Boston: Little, Brown and Company.

Kirby, William C (2015) "The real reason Uber is giving up in China." *Harvard Business Review* 2 (2016).

Kirkham, Elyssa (2020) "Chase Student Loans Are Gone – Here's What To Do Instead." studentloanhero.com, published online on January 24, 2020 https://studentloanhero.com/featured/chase-student-loans-happened/

Krawiec, K. D. (2013). "Don't Screw Joe the Plummer: The Sausage-Making of Financial Reform." *Arizona Law Review* 55, 53.

Krawiec, Kimberly D., and Guangya Liu. (2015) "The Volcker Rule: a brief political history." *Capital Markets Law Journal* 10.4: 507–522.

Kurzban, Robert, Peter DeScioli, and Erin O'Brien (2007) "Audience effects on moralistic punishment." *Evolution and Human Behavior* 28.2 (2007): 75–84.

Kwak, James. (2014). "Cultural capture and the financial crisis." In *Preventing regulatory capture: Special interest influence and how to limit it* 71 (2014): 79–81.

LaVito, Angelica (2019a) "Sixth person dies from vaping-linked lung disease." CNBC.com, published Sept 10 2019 at 1:08 PM.

LaVito, Angelica (2019b) "CDC says teen vaping surges to more than 1 in 4 high school students." CNBC.com, published Sept 12 2019 at 10:53 AM.

Le, Stefanie (2019) "How NYC Learned to Stop Worrying about Ride-Hailing Services and Utilize Data." Ash Center for Democratic Governance and Innovation, weblog page posted: 2019-11-25 https://datasmart.ash.harvard.edu/news/article/how-nyc-learned-stop-worrying-about-ride-hailing-services-and-utilize -data

Leetaru, Kalev (2021) "Biden's First 100 Days: Extending A Freeze On Student Loan Payments." RealClear Politics, posted on April 9, 2021 www .realclearpolitics.com/video/2021/04/09/bidens_first_100_days_extending_a_ freeze_on_student_loan_payments.html

Looney, Adam, David Wessel, and Kadija Yilla (2020) "Who owes all that student debt? And who'd benefit if it were forgiven?" The Brooking Institution, published online on January 28, 2020 www.brookings.edu/policy2020/votervital/who-owes-all-that-student-debt-and-whod-benefit-if-it-were-forgiven/

Lucchetti, Aaron and Paletta, Damian (2010) "Lobbyists Can't Get in Door." *Wall Street Journal June* 14, 2010.

Lunden, Ingrid (2012) "Uber's Travis Kalanick On Regulators: You Have To Grit Your Teeth, Be A Warrior, Or Do Something Less Disruptive." TechCrunch.com, published online at 12:41 PM CDT, September 12, 2012. https://techcrunch.com/2012/09/12/ubers-travis-kalanick-on-regulators-you-have-to-grit-your-teeth-be-a-warrior-or-do-something-less-disruptive/

Mahoney, Christine, and Frank R. Baumgartner (2015) "Partners in advocacy: lobbyists and government officials in Washington." *The Journal of Politics* 77.1 (2015): 202–215.

McNutt, Marcia K., Rich Camilli, Timothy J. Crone, George D. Guthrie, Paul A. Hsieh, Thomas B. Ryerson, Omer Savas, Frank Shaffer (2012) "Review of flow rate estimates of the Deepwater Horizon oil spill." *Proceedings of the National Academy of Sciences* Dec 2012, 109 (50) 20260–20267; DOI: 10.1073/pnas.1112139108

Meixel, Antonie, Elena Yanchar, and Adriane Fugh-Berman (2015) "Hypoactive Sexual Desire Disorder: Inventing a Disease to Sell Low Libido." *Journal of Medical Ethics* 41, no. 10 (2015): 859–62. www.jstor.org/stable/44014232.

Michigan News (2021) "Current focus on preventing youth vaping could hinder adults' efforts to stop smoking." August 19, 2021. https://news.umich.edu/current-focus-on-preventing-youth-vaping-could-hinder-adults-efforts-to-stop-smoking/

Miller, Matthew (2022) "Jordan Peterson says Joe Rogan beats ratings of legacy media because 'he doesn't lie" Washington Examiner, January 07, 2022 11:53 AM www.washingtonexaminer.com/news/jordan-peterson-says-joe-rogan-beats-ratings-of-legacy-media-because-he-doesnt-lie

Minor and Persico (2012) "The Volcker Rule: Financial Crisis, Bailouts, and the Need for Financial Regulation," Kellogg Case # 5-412-753, Nov 5, 2012.

Mintz, John (1995) "Criticism Leveled at the NRA" The Washington Post, April 28, 1995 www.washingtonpost.com/archive/politics/1995/04/28/criticism-leveled-at-the-nra/7d8c1769-4acb-4a96-845a-0c5ef6775f22/

Moynihan, Ray (2003) "The making of a disease: female sexual dysfunction." *British Medical Journal* 326.7379 (2003): 45–47.

Muck Rack (2021) "The State of Journalism 2021 Survey." https://muckrack .com/blog/2021/03/15/state-of-journalism-2021

Muir, David, and Joel Siegel (2009) "Former Sen. Max Cleland Details Political War Wounds in Memoir: Post-Traumatic Stress Syndrome." ABC News, published online on December 11, 2009, 5:07 PM. https://abcnews.go.com/WN/sen-max-cleland-details-political-war-wounds-post/story?id=9315832

Müller, W.C. (2000) "Political parties in parliamentary democracies: Making delegation and accountability work." *European Journal of Political Research* 37: 309–333. https://doi.org/10.1023/A:1007073021074

Nakamura, Leonard I., Jon Samuels, and Rachel H. Soloveichik (2017) "Measuring the 'Free' Digital Economy within the GDP and productivity accounts." Bureau of Economic Analysis working paper. www.bea.gov/research/papers/2017/measuring-free-digital-economy-within-gdp-and-productivity -accounts

National Organization for Women (2015) "National Organization for Women Welcomes FDA Decision on Women's HSDD Treatment." Now.org, Released on August 19, 2015 https://now.org/media-center/press-release/national-organization-for-women-welcomes-fda-decision-on-womens-hsdd-treatment/

NRA-ILA (2022) "Pro-Gun Members of Congress Demand Answers from ATF on Mass Suppressor Application Denials." NRA-ILA.org, published online on March 28, 2022. www.nraila.org/articles/20220328/pro-gun-members-of-congress-demand-answers-from-atf-on-mass-suppressor-application-denials

Obama, Barak (2010, January 21) "Full Text of Obama's Remarks on Financial Reform." The Wall Street Journal. https://wsj.com/articles/BL-DLB-19433

OpenSecrets (2022) "Lobbying Data Summary," accessed March 17, 2022. www.opensecrets.org/federal-lobbying

Papper, Bob (2016) "RTDNA Research: Newsroom salary survey." June 27, 2016, www.rtdna.org/article/rtdna_research_newsroom_salary_survey

Park-Lee E, Ren C, Sawdey MD, et al. (2021) "Notes from the Field: E-Cigarette Use Among Middle and High School Students — National Youth Tobacco Survey, United States, 2021." MMWR Morb Mortal Wkly Rep 2021;70:1387–1389. DOI: http://dx.doi.org/10.15585/mmwr.mm7039a4.

Pentis, Andrew "The History of Student Loans (and How to Avoid Repeating It)" Studentloanhero.com, published online on June 25, 2021 https://studentloanhero.com/featured/history-student-loans/

Persico, Nicola, Andrew Postlewaite, and Dan Silverman (2003) "The effect of adolescent experience on labor market outcomes: The case of height." *Journal of Political Economy* 112.5 (2004): 1019–1053.

Persico, Nicola, and C. James Prieur (2017) "Conseco Senior Health Insurance: A Strategic Problem of Reputation and Regulation." Kellogg School of Management Cases (2017).

Pew Research Center (2021) "Public Trust in Government: 1958–2021." Feature, May 17, 2021 www.pewresearch.org/politics/2021/05/17/public-trust-in-government-1958-2021/

Pew Research Center (2022), June 2022, "Americans' Views of Government: Decades of Distrust, Enduring Support for Its Role" www.pewresearch.org/politics/2022/06/06/americans-views-of-government-decades-of-distrust-enduring-support-for-its-role/

Pinetree (2019) "U.S. Newsroom Employment Dropped 25% Since 2008, Newspapers Down 47%." Published July 10, 2019 8:20 am, http://thepinetree.net/new/?p=83150

Priest, Tyler (2010). "The ties that bind MMS and big oil." Politico (2010).

Public Papers of the Presidents of the United States. (2010a). "Remarks at Celgard, LLC, April 2, 2010." United States: Federal Register Division, National Archives and Records Service, General Services Administration.

Public Papers of the Presidents of the United States. (2010b). "Address to the Nation on the Oil Spill in the Gulf of Mexico, June 15, 2010." United States: Federal Register Division, National Archives and Records Service, General Services Administration.

Public Papers of the Presidents of the United States. (1962). "The President's News Conference of August 1, 1962." United States: Federal Register Division, National Archives and Records Service, General Services Administration.

Quorum (2018) "Enacted Bills with Bipartisan Support at 20-Year High." Available at www.quorum.us/data-driven-insights/may-2018-congressional-activity-report/

Rivkin, Charles H. (2018) "CEO Letter." Accessed at https://50th.filmratings.com/core/ on Jan 24, 2022.

Saad, Lydia (2022) "Military Brass, Judges Among Professions at New Image Lows." Gallup Online, published January 12, 2022 https://news.gallup.com/poll/388649/military-brass-judges-among-professions-new-image-lows.aspx

Sanchez, Humberto (2012) "Internet Piracy Bills Lose Support." Roll Call, Posted January 18, 2012 at 7:53pm. https://rollcall.com/2012/01/18/internet-piracy-bills-lose-support/

Severns, Maggie (2013) "The Student Loan Debt Crisis in 9 Charts." Mother Jones, published June 5, 2013, www.motherjones.com/politics/2013/06/student-loan-debt-charts/

Shohov, Tatiana, ed. (2004) Federal student loans. Nova Publishers, 2004.

Smart, Rosanna, and Terry L. Schell (2021). "Mass shootings in the United States." The RAND Corporation (2021) www.rand.org/research/gun-policy/analysis/essays/mass-shootings.html

Small, Deborah A., George Loewenstein, and Paul Slovic (2007). "Sympathy and callousness: The impact of deliberative thought on donations to identifiable and statistical victims." Organizational Behavior and Human Decision Processes 102.2 (2007): 143–153.

Smith, Brad, and Carol Ann Browne (2021) Tools and weapons: The promise and the peril of the digital age. Penguin, 2021.

Smith, Timothy and John Keenan (2018) "Disclosing Corporate Lobbying." Posted on Monday, April 2, 2018 https://corpgov.law.harvard.edu/2018/04/02/disclosing-corporate-lobbying/

Spenkuch, Jörg, Edoardo Teso, and Guo Xu "Ideology and Performance in Public Organizations." Manuscript, November 24, 2021.

The White House (2011) "Ensuring That Student Loans are Affordable" available online at https://obamawhitehouse.archives.gov/issues/education/higher-education/ensuring-that-student-loans-are-affordable

Theriot, Stuart (2014) "Changing Direction: How Regulatory Agencies Have Responded to the Deepwater Horizon Oil Spill." *LSU Journal of Energy Law & Resources Currents* (November 19, 2014). http://sites.law.lsu.edu/jelrblog/?p=506.

Tilley, Aaron, and Ryan Tracy (2020) "How Microsoft Became Washington's Favorite Tech Giant." *The Wall Street Journal*, April 2, 2022 12:04 am ET www.wsj.com/articles/how-microsoft-became-washingtons-favorite-tech-giant-11648872240

TobaccoTactics (2022) "JUUL Labs," University of Bath, https://tobaccotactics.org/wiki/juul-labs/. Last edited on 13 January 2022, at 6:44 am.

Tracy, Ryan (2020) "Big Tech's Power Comes Under Fire at Congressional Antitrust Hearing." *The Wall Street Journal*, April 29, 2020 7:29 pm ET www.wsj.com/articles/tech-ceos-defend-operations-ahead-of-congressional-hearing-11596027626?mod=article_inline

Trebbi, Francesco, and Kairong Xiao (2019) "Regulation and Market Liquidity." *Management Science* 65(5):1949–1968.

Vizzard, William J. (1995) "The impact of agenda conflict on policy formulation and implementation: The case of gun control." *Public Administration Review* (1995): 341–347.

Waldmeir, Patti. (2015) "China outlines regulations for car-hailing apps such as Uber." CNBC, published Oct. 11, 2015 at 5:02 AM EDT. www.cnbc.com/2015/10/11/china-outlines-regulations-for-car-hailing-apps-uber-didi-kuaidi.html

Wang, Quan-Jing, Gen-Fu Feng, Hai-Jie Wang, and Chun-Ping Chang (2012) "The impacts of democracy on innovation: Revisited evidence." *Technovation* 108 (2021): 102333.

Washington, Ebonya L. (2008) "Female socialization: how daughters affect their legislator fathers." *American Economic Review* 98.1 (2008): 311–32.

Watts, Geoff (2015) "Frances Oldham Kelsey." *The Lancet* 386.10001 (2015): 1334.

Weisman, Jonathan (2012) "After an Online Firestorm, Congress Shelves Antipiracy Bills." *The New York Times*, Jan. 20, 2012.

Wilson, Elliot "Can the Cowboy State sell crypto to the Fed?" Euromoney online, February 25, 2022 www.euromoney.com/article/29rem175z7iw1vgd6zbpc/fintech/can-the-cowboy-state-sell-crypto-to-the-fed

WIPO (2021). *Global Innovation Index 2021: Tracking Innovation through the COVID-19 Crisis*. Geneva: World Intellectual Property Organization.

Wolters Kluwer (2013) "2013 CCH Whole Ball of Tax: A Historical Look at Top Marginal Income Tax Rates." www.cch.com/wbot2013/029IncomeTaxRates.asp

Wouters OJ. (2020) "Lobbying Expenditures and Campaign Contributions by the Pharmaceutical and Health Product Industry in the United States, 1999–2018." *JAMA Internal Medicine* 2020;180(5):688–697.

Yackee, Susan Webb (2014). "Reconsidering agency capture during regulatory policymaking." In *Preventing regulatory capture: Special interest influence and how to limit it* (2014): 292–325.

Yackee, Susan Webb (2019) "The Politics of Rulemaking in the United States." *Annual Review of Political Science* 22:37–55 (Volume publication date May 2019) https://doi.org/10.1146/annurev-polisci-050817-092302

York, Erica (2021) "2022 Tax Brackets." Tax Foundation, published online on November 10, 2021 https://taxfoundation.org/publications/federal-tax-rates-and-tax-brackets/#: :text=The%20top%20marginal%20income%20tax,for%20married%20couples%20filing%20jointly.

Zahariadis, Nikolaos. (2019). "The multiple streams framework: Structure, limitations, prospects." In Theories of the policy process (pp. 65–92). Routledge.

Index

Printed in the United States
by Baker & Taylor Publisher Services